TARBERT

IN

PICTURE   AND   STORY

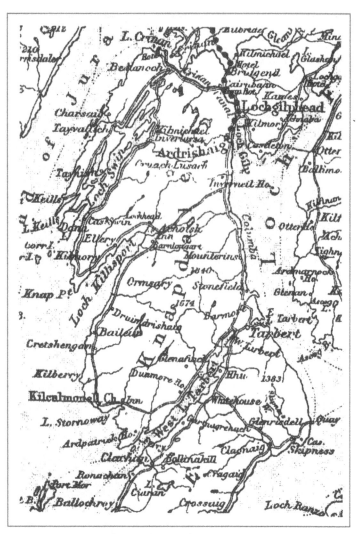

MAP OF TARBERT AND DISTRICT.

TARBERT

IN

PICTURE AND STORY

BY

DUGALD MITCHELL, M.D.

AUTHOR OF "THE HISTORY OF THE HIGHLANDS AND GAELIC SCOTLAND."

First Published

FALKIRK:

JOHN CALLANDER, HIGH STREET

1908

This edition published in 2018 by
Birlinn Origin, an imprint of
Birlinn Limited
West Newington House
10 Newington Road
Edinburgh
EH9 1QS

www.birlinn.co.uk

First published in 1908 by John Callander, Falkirk

ISBN 978 1 91247 618 3
eBook ISBN 978 1 78885 126 8

British Library Cataloguing-in-Publication Data
A catalogue record for this book is available
from the British Library

Typeset by Geethik Technologies, India
Printed and bound by Clays Ltd, Elcograf S.p.A

CONTENTS.

Contents

THE AUTHOR BEGS TO THANK MESSRS WM. RITCHIE & SONS, LTD., EDINBURGH, FOR PERMISSION TO USE PHOTOGRAPHS ON PAGES 69 AND 99; AND MESSRS VALENTINE & SONS, LTD., DUNDEE, FOR THE SAME PRIVILEGE AS REGARDS TO PHOTOGRAPH ON PAGE 67.

A SONG OF TARBERT.

CHORUS—Oh, my home, my Highland home!
     O'er thy hills I long to roam;
     Oh, my dear old Highland home
       I'll ever love thee, Tarbert.

Oh, could I wander by thy shore,
Or sail thy shadowy waters o'er;
Alas! I never see thee more,
   I never see thee, Tarbert.

I long to watch the moonbeams play
On shimmering loch and castle gray;
Or linger where the burnies stray
   Adown thy fair hills, Tarbert.

Oh, lone Maoldarach, green Barfad!
Thy sunny memories make me glad;
And every beathery brae I tread
   Awakens thoughts of Tarbert.

How off I've sought Glenralloch's shade
With thee, my winsome Highland maid;
Or round the woody Carrick strayed,
   By bonnie West Loch Tarbert.

I've wandered east, I've wandered west,
And strayed far from my Highland nest
But, ah! the place that I love best
   Is just the home at Tarbert.

TARBERT

IN

PICTURE AND STORY.

QUAINT and picturesque in its surroundings, there is in this old village, which nestles so cosily in its setting of hills, much to charm and much to interest. Its story, as we shall see, brings it in touch with many of the leading events in our nation's history, while its breezy fisher life, and its unadorned natural features, with all that

THE HAVEN UNDER THE HILL.

these imply—the freedom of its heath-clad hills, the restful silences of its solitary glens, its sheltered, rocky bay, and the contrasting western loch, smiling among its softer, sylvan beauties—lend to it an attractiveness all its own among the sea-side resorts of the west. It is our purpose to tell that story, and to illustrate some of the most characteristic features of the village and its neighbourhood.

The place-name "Tarbert" is probably, in one or other of its forms, the commonest in Scotland. It is interesting to note in the literature of the centuries the varied spellings of the name in relation to Tarbert Loch Fyne alone. In the oldest records it appears as *Tairpirt.* Soon it takes the form of *Tarbart* and *Tarbard,* and later it appears indiscriminately as *Terbert, Tarbert, Tarbett, Tarbet, Tarbatt, Tarbat, Torban, Tarbot, Tarbitt, Terbat, Turbet,* and *Terbart.*

The derivation of the name has been frequently a matter of controversy. Among Gaelic people the term almost invariably used in speaking of Tarbert is *An Tairbeart—i.e.,* "The Tarbert," by which

THE CASTLE HILL.

is almost certainly meant a narrow neck of land or isthmus—that natural feature which is, in fact, characteristic of all the places bearing the name Tarbert or Tarbet. The component parts of the word may be found in *tar,* signifying "across," and *bert,* of the verb *beir* "carry," a place across which things are carried, "a portage"; or, they may be found in the words *tearb aird,* signifying "a separating rising ground," a neck of land separating two waters. The latter represents the more primitive form of nomenclature, and best characterises the natural feature, but either derivation may be considered satisfactory.

Links with the Days of Old.

Tarbert has many links, traditional and historic, which interestingly associate it with the memories of ruder and stormier times. In some of the most

The Story of Diarmaid and Grainne

beautiful spots in the neighbourhood "the sun-worshipping" Druid had made his home, and here and there his noble dead are commemorated by old gray monolith or standing stone. The proud legionaries of Rome, it is not improbable, trod its isthmus pathway in A.D. 82, when, with a view to future conquests in the sister isle, Agricola sailed down the Firth and "placed forces in that part of Britain which fronts Ireland." It shared in those periodic incursions of the Scots from Ireland, which culminated (498-501) in the definite seizure of Kintyre, the sea-board of Argyle, and many of the Western Isles by Loarn, and Angus, and Fergus Mor, the founders of the Scottish kingdom of Dalriada. And it shared in the more peaceful conquest of St. Columba and his fellow-soldiers of the Cross. Through the ministry of St. Colman Ela, who is still commemorated in the parish name "Kilcalmonell," and of St. Cormack, whose name continues to live in the place-name "Kilchamaig" or "Kilcharmaig," North Kintyre was early brought under Christian influences. In the many chapels which were dotted over the district the lamp was ever kept burning and, though we cannot now trace their footsteps, saints many held the neighbourhood in close touch with Iona and Ireland, as they passed and re-passed over Tarbert's narrow isthmus on their mission of love.

Tradition associates North Kintyre and Knapdale with the romantic story of Diarmaid and Grainne, a story which carries us back to the days of the great Fingalian heroes. It is to be said, however, that there are many versions of the story, both in prose and verse, and the scene of action is varied, and not limited even to Scotland. Of all the so-called Ossianic poems this is one of the most popular, and one of the earliest to appear in literature. The version we follow runs shortly thus:—

Grainne, daughter of an Irish king, the faithless bride of Finn or Fingal, and the Guinevere of ancient Gaelic story, fell madly in love, ere yet her wedding festivities were over, with Diarmaid O'Duibhne, the brown-haired, blue-eyed, gay and gallant nephew of Fingal. She had looked, as it chanced, upon the fair brow of Diarmaid, with its *ball seirc*, or love spot, which no woman could once see without instantly losing her heart to him!

3

Tarbert

Unable long to resist the entreaties of Grainne—for the whisper of a woman's love in his ear was ever to Diarmaid the sweetest of sounds—the lovers fled from Ireland to Kintyre. At Carraig-an-Daimh, near Kilchamaig (seven miles from Tarbert), the unfaithful Grainne—unfaithful still—fell in love with Old Ciofach Mac a Ghoill (the son of the stranger), whom Diarmaid slew after a determined struggle.

Leaving Kintyre, Diarmaid proceeded to the great mountain ridge of Sliabh Gaoil, the "Hill of Love," immediately to the north of Tarbert, whence he was followed by Grainne. After a time, fearing capture by Fingal, they fled north to Glenelg, where, according to the version followed up to this point, Diarmaid, on the challenge of Fingal, slew the dreaded wild boar; and, later, the outraged husband had his revenge.* And this was the manner of the revenge:—

> " 'O Diarmaid! measure the boar,' he said,
>   'With thy bare feet, for great is his size';
> He measured the boar with the bristles,
>   Sixteen good feet where he lies.
>
> 'O Diarmaid! measure him back again;
>   He is not so much,' Finn cries.
> He measures him back, and a poisonous bristle
>   Pierces his foot as he tries.
>
> .   .   .   .
>
> Beneath thy grey stones, O Ben Goolbain
>   The brown-haired chief is laid;
> His blue eyes are sleeping forever
>   Under thy green grassy shade. "†

Local tradition associates the great hunt and the death of Diarmaid with the neighbourhood of Tarbert, and it is interesting to note that three places in Kintyre and Knapdale bear names which are appropriate to the tale. From *Ben-an-Tuirc*, "the Mountain of the Boar" (near Saddell), Diarmaid, so runs the local story, pursued the chase through glen and over hill to *Leum-na-Muic*, "the Pig's Leap" (near Loupe), where two rocks are shown, across which the boar leapt. Thence the bold hunter urged the chase round the head of West Loch Tarbert, till eventually the boar was slain on *Torr-an-Tuirc*, "The Boar's Heap,"

* "Popular Tales of the West Highlands," vol. iii. p. 49.
† Pattison's "Gaelic Bards," p. 180.

a spur of the Sliabh Gaoil range on the right of the Kilberry road, and about four miles from Tarbert.

But, as has been already hinted, the bones of the monster boar are in many a cairn over the west and north!

Diarmaid O'Duibhne, after whom the Campbells are traditionally known as Siol Diarmaid or Clan O'Duine, is the mythical ancestor of that great family, and the Argyll branch bear the boar's head as their crest. We may take it as an historic fact that there has been a real Diarmaid among the early progenitors of the clan, one in whose honour poems have been written and tales told; but the characteristics attributed to him are mythical, and belong to a still earlier period in the history of the world.

THE DAY OF REST.

The Strategic Importance of the Isthmus.

The historic associations of Tarbert centre largely around military events. This we might expect from the strategical importance of its geographical position, commanding, as it does, the shortest and the safest route between the Western Islands and the Firth of Clyde.

There is reason to believe that from a very early period a fort or place of strength crowned its castle-hill. In the stormy days of the Dalriadic kingdom such a structure did exist some-where in the neighbourhood, as we learn from the old "Annals of

Ulster," which record that on two occasions (712 and 731) a fort at Tarbert was burned by the usurping King Selbach and his equally vigorous and ambitious son, who was known as Dungal the Violent.* In the meagre entries which record these events we find the first historic references to Tarbert. The good old town is therefore no child of yesterday, and we may have no difficulty in concluding that many a warlike, though unrecorded event, centred around its isthmus and its fort in those rude and far-off days.

"As on dry land the galley moves,
By cliff, and copse, and alder groves."

The centuries pass, and Tarbert next appears upon the page of history in the year 1093, when the chief actor was Magnus Barefoot, King of Norway, who is thus referred to by Carlyle in quaint and characteristic phrase: "This son [of Olaf the Tranquil] bears the name of Magnus *Burfod* (Barefoot or Bareleg); and, if you ask why so, the answer is: He was used to appear in the streets of Nidaros (Trondhjem) now and then in complete Scotch Highland dress. Authentic tartan plaid and philibeg, at that period,—to the wonder of Trondhjem and us! The truth is, he had a mighty fancy for those Hebrides and other Scotch possessions of his. . . ." At the time of which Carlyle writes, plaid and kilt were all of a piece, so we fear that in the matter of the "philibeg" our distinguished author is a little at fault.

The incident referred to illustrates well this "fancy" of Magnus for Scotch possessions. According to the Saga he had made a treaty with the Scottish king, in terms of which "King Magnus should have all the islands that lie to the West of Scotland—all of them, to wit, betwixt which and the mainland a keel, with rudder shipped, could fare. But when King Magnus came from the south up to Cantire, then let he drag a cutter over Cantire-neck [Santiri-eidhs], with rudder shipped, and himself sat on the poop and held the tiller; and thus got he to

* The phrase used in the "Annals" on both occasions is *Combustio Tairpirt Boetter.* It has been found impossible to definitely determine the meaning of the word "Boetter," but it is almost certain that a fort of some kind is meant.

him so much land as lay to larboard. Cantire is a mickle land, and better than the best isle of the South Isles, save Man. A narrow neck there is between it and the mainland of Scotland, and thereover long ships are often dragged."

Principal Shairp gave a poetic setting to the story in "Kilmahoe":—

> "Then Norroway kings, our chiefs o'erthrown,
> Held isle and islet for their own,
>   And one, more haughty than the rest,
> Swore he would claim for island ground
> Whate'er he drove his galley round;
>   And from the Atlantic, up the west
> Loch Tarbert bearing, made them haul
> His barge across that isthmus small;
>   Himself proud seated at the helm.
> Then spreading sail down fair Lochfyne,
> He cried aloud, 'Kintyre is mine,
>   I've bound it to my island realm.'"

CROSSING THE BAY.

The exploit was picturesque, but the transaction was transparently fraudulent—"a guileful interpretation" of the treaty—and it may be surmised that King Malcolm Ceannmor was not in a position to successfully intervene in these somewhat remote parts, or such an unwarranted seizure of a valuable portion of the mainland would surely have called forth the most determined resistance on the part of this energetic king. From an early period, and until the seventeenth century, Kintyre was reckoned one of the South Isles, or Sudreys; but whether or not on account of this incident we cannot tell.

In his "Early Kings of Norway," from which we have already quoted, Carlyle refers to a somewhat similar incident as having occurred in the same situation in 1263, when Haco of Norway was on his way to the Firth of Clyde in that memorable invasion of his which culminated in the Battle of Largs. Quoting and commenting as he goes, Carlyle writes thus: "While his ships and army were doubling the Mull of Cantyre he had his own boat set on wheels, and therein, splendidly enough, had himself drawn across the Promontory at a flatter part," no doubt with horns sounding, banners waving. "'All to the left of me is mine and Norway's,' exclaimed Hakon in his triumphant boat progress, which such disasters soon followed." The story reads like an echo of the Magnus Barefoot exploit, and no reference to such an incident is made in the Flateyan and Frisian MSS., which give a strikingly minute account of the voyage and the battle. According to these records, Haco, after remaining a considerable time at Gigha, where he had interviews with the Abbot of Saddell and Eogan, the chief of the M'Dougalls, or King John as he is called in the Saga, "sailed south before the Mull of Kintyre with all his fleet; a mighty and splendid armament, the mightiest, it is said, that ever left these northern shores." It consisted of upward of 120 sail, carrying twenty thousand men.

In these MSS. the dealings of King Haco with the chiefs of Kintyre, Islay, and others of the Western Isles are interestingly described, and we are given to see the difficulties these chiefs lay under in the matter of allegiance, on the one hand to the King of Scotland, and on the other to the King of Norway.

But their time of deliverance from the over-lordship of Norway had now come, for Haco was the last of his race to rule the western seas. Passing through Kyle Akin (Haco) in his inglorious return towards his northern home, the broken-hearted king landed on Orkney, where he died in the Bishop's Palace at Kirkwall.

> "And they laid thee, Haco, Haco,
>   With thy sires on the Norway shore,
> And far from the isles of the sea, Haco,
>   That know thy name no more."

A Tradition of Sliabh Gaoil

The Wanderings of the Bruce.

Relieved thus and forever from the frequent harassments of the Northern Power, Scotland soon found herself called upon to engage her whole energies in repelling the presumption of her Southern neighbour. In connection with this great struggle Cuthbert Bede, in his "Glencreggan," records the following tradition, which brings Bruce (in 1306) over Sliabh Gaoil, the hill of the mythical Diarmaid and Grainne, and across the isthmus into Kintyre, after his encounter with the Mac Dougalls and their allies at Dalry, near Tyndrum. It was in this melee, as will be remembered, that the King's plaid was torn from his shoulders, and with it the brooch since known as the Brooch of Lorn—

> "Wrought and chased with rare device,
> Studded fair with gems of price."

"On the bleak mountain," says Bede, "in South Knapdale, called Sliabh Gaoil, the hunted monarch passed a cheerless night. He was well nigh spent with fatigue and hunger, and, to add to his distress, the night was bitterly cold. He would, probably, have perished had

RECALMED.

not a goat come to him, and laid herself down beside him. She suffered him to refresh himself with her milk, and kept him warm all the night through. Refreshed by the night's rest, and the goat's milk and warmth, the Bruce came on to Cantyre the next morning. It was in grateful

9

memory of this that when 'he enjoyed his own agen,' he made a law that forbade any one to poind (or pound) a goat."

It seems a pity to lower such picturesque traditions in popular regard, but it is to be feared that this one gains no support from

THE CASTLE FROM THE PIER ROAD.

historical probabilities. Barbour, in his "Brus," brings the fugitive king from the shores of the Firth of Clyde to Saddell in boats provided by the staunch patriot, Sir Niel Campbell, ancestor of the Argyll family. There he was warmly received by Angus Oig, the chief of the Kintyre Mac Donalds, and younger brother of Alexander of Islay, Lord of the Isles. From Saddell, Bruce passed to the Castle of Dunaverty, and thence to Rathlin, the scene of the never-to-be-forgotten spider story, which has ever since placed that persevering and industrious insect on a high pinnacle in the regard of self-respecting boyhood.

He "gert his schippis with saillis ga,
Out our betwix the Tarbartis twa."

Eight years later (1314) Bannockburn was fought, and Scotland was free.

The task which the King now found before him of introducing order into his long-troubled dominions

was one of no light nature, and this it will be readily understood
was more particularly true of the Highlands and Western Isles. In
the year 1315, after his brother Edward had entered on his ill-starred
struggle for the Irish crown, Bruce's attention was directed to John
of Lorn, the chief of the Mac Dougalls, Alexander of Islay, and other
Western chiefs who were acting at that time as the allies of England.
In his journey to the west he chose the route across the isthmus of
Tarbert. According to Barbour, who gives a highly picturesque and
quaint description of the scene, the land journey over the isthmus was
performed on a primitive ship-railway constructed for the purpose.
The distance between the two lochs was "lompnyt all with treis."
Taking advantage of a favourable wind that was blowing, the galleys
were placed on the structure, all the sails were set, the men put to
work, and so, by means of this unique combination of sailing and
hauling on dry land, the western loch was reached.

Barbour's lines run thus:—

"When he had conwoyit to the se
His brodyr Eduuard, and his menye,
With his shippis he maid him yare
Into the Ilis for to fayr.
Walter Stewart with him tuk he,
His maich, and with him gret menye;
And othyr men off gret noblay.
To Tarbart thai held thair way,
In galayis ordanyt for thair far.
Bot thaim worthyt draw thair schippis thar:
And a myle was betwix the seys;
But that was lompnyt all with treis.
The king his schippis thar gert draw.
And for the wynd couth stoutly blaw
Apon thair bak, as thai wald ga,
He gert men rapys and mastis ta,
And set thaim in the schippis hey,
And sayllis to the toppis tey;
And gert men gang thar by drawand.
The wynd thaim helpyt, that was blawand;
Swa that, in a litill space,
Thair flote all our drawin was.

And quhen thai, that in the Ilis war,
Hard tell how the gud king had thar
Gort his schippis with saillis ga,
Owt our betwix [the] Tarbart [is] twa,
Thai war abaysit sa wtrely.
For thai wyst, throw auld prophecy,
That be that suld ger schippis sua
Betuix thai seis with saillis ga,

11

Suld wyne the Ilis sua till band,
That nane with strenth sold him withstand.
Tharfor thai come all to the king.
Wes nane withstud his bidding,
Owtakyn Jhone of Lorne allayne.
Bot weill sone eftre was he tayne. "

The "auld prophecy" here referred to, which had so powerfully impressed the minds of the Islesmen as to have brought almost all of them to the feet of the king, probably had for its foundation the successful stratagem of Magnus Barefoot more than two centuries before. There is a tradition that during the transference over the isthmus one of the ships came to grief at *Lag-Luinge*, "ship hollow," so called from this incident.

Sir Walter Scott, in his "Lord of the Isles," makes use of the above incident, and, applying it to an earlier date, describes an imaginary journey of the Bruce across the isthmus, when on his way from Rathlin to Arran in 1307:—

"Ever the breeze blows merrily,
But the galley ploughs no more the sea.
Lest rounding wild Cantire they meet
The southern foeman's watchful fleet,
    They held unwonted way;—
Up Tarbat's western lake they bore,
Then dragged their bark the isthmus o'er.
As far as Kilmaconnel's shore,
    Upon the eastern bay.
It was a wondrous sight to see
Topmast and pennon glitter free
High raised above the greenwood tree,
As on dry land the galley moves,
By cliff and copse and alder groves.
Deep import from that selcouth sign,
Did many a mountain seer divine,
For ancient legends told the Gael,
That when a royal bark should sail
    O'er Kilmaconnel moss,
Old Albyn should in fight prevail,
And every foe should faint and quail
    Before her silver Cross. "

"High on the crag serenely stands
The towering castle grim and gray. "

The old castle, hoary and time-worn, the most striking feature in the surrounding landscape, is the

The Castle of the Bruce

most prized of Tarbert's possessions. It is, indeed, difficult to think of Tarbert without it. The centuries have told their tale of inevitable decay upon its structure, and particularly upon its older parts; but this interesting link with the past still stands proudly against the sky, a stately and picturesque ruin.

Occupying a commanding site, it must have been in the hey-day of its power almost impregnable, and eminently fitted to overawe the country around, and to serve as a convenient base of operations from which to keep the Islesmen in check. These, in fact, were its functions from the time it first appears upon the page of history towards the close of the thirteenth century, when it was a royal castle. How long before that date a fort or castle crowned the height there is nothing to show, but it is highly probable, as we have seen, that, whether as a possession of the Crown or of a Highland chief, a site which was of such strategic importance would have been occupied by a fortified strength from a very early period.

Whatever may have been the character and extent of the castle before 1325, Bruce began very extensive operations upon it in that year. His previous visits to the neighbourhood would, doubtless, have impressed upon him the desirability of guarding the isthmus as effectively as possible.

The interest attaching to these operations of the "Good King" is enormously enhanced by the important circumstance that many details regarding them were furnished in the year 1326 by John De Lany, the then Constable of Tarbert, and are still extant. These constitute, according to the editors of the "Origines Parochiales Scotiæ," "the earliest account of any details of domestic architecture and modes of rural life in Scotland." Indeed, the earliest Scottish Exchequer Roll in existence is that contributed by the Constable of Tarbert, all earlier ones having been destroyed or lost during the Wars of Independence. In the original Latin, this interesting document may be found in the "Exchequer Rolls of Scotland" and in the "Compota Cameraria Scotiæ," while an English translation of the greater portion is given in the "Origines Parochiales Scotiæ."

A perusal of the following elaborate and complete description of the buildings, which we are privileged to quote here in full from a most valuable work,* shows to us very clearly and interestingly the need there was for the revision of local and popular opinion as to the extent and character of the structure, and as to the identity of the builders of the different portions. From this scientific description we learn that the castle of Bruce was a much larger building than it has popularly, and within these later times, been supposed to be. Its foundations are traced in the large square to the west of the keep, which is locally known as the "barracks," and, if we picture to ourselves the walls that are there represented carried to a height of two or three stories, as they probably were, we can see that the main building was indeed of very considerable dimensions.

THE KEEP FROM THE N.W.

The keep, on the other hand, which alone has been traditionally considered to be the "castle," and to have been built by Bruce, belongs to a later period, and is almost certainly the work of James IV. towards the end of the fifteenth century. These and other points of very great interest are very clearly

* The Castellated and Domestic Architecture of Scotland from the Twelfth to the Eighteenth Century, by David MacGibbon and Thomas Ross, Architects, 1887.

Description of the Historic Ruin

brought out in the description referred to, which runs as follows:—

"This castle is of unusual interest from being intimately associated with King Robert the Bruce. It is situated on a small creek called Loch Tarbert, on the west side of Loch Fyne, and stands on an eminence about 60 feet above the sea, and at a distance from the shore of about 60 yards. It was one of the royal fortresses which Edward I. caused to be handed over to Baliol, after placing him on the throne in 1292. In 1325 Bruce had the castle inspected and repaired, with the intention of using it for the purpose of overawing the Highlanders, then being brought by him under subjection, and a glance at the map will show that the situation of Tarbert on its isthmus is one of the best strategical positions in the country. The object of the castle from its first erection must have been to serve as an entrenched camp or stronghold for a large garrison on the edge of a country which might any day rise up in rebellion, and this explains its plan. The castle with which Bruce's name is associated seems hitherto not to have been recognised, but has always been confounded with a late keep adjoining it to the east, situated in the outer courtyard. It is shown by hatched lines on the plan (page 16), and will be hereafter described.

We have now no means of exactly determining to what extent the castle existed before Bruce's additions and repairs were made, but judging by analogy, we may infer that the square enclosure which constitutes the castle proper was what he found existing before he commenced his operations. This castle or enclosure has a strong resemblance to Kinclaven Castle, Perthshire, a pre-Brucian castle of almost the same size and plan. If this surmise is correct, we may conclude that Bruce erected the lower court with its drum towers, and so enlarged the castle as to make it better available for his purpose.

TARBERT CASTLE

consisted of walls enclosing a square measuring about 120 feet each way, now generally reduced to little more than grass mounds, with pieces of masonry seen here and there, except along the north-east curtain, where considerable portions of the old wall can still be seen on the lower ground outside. These walls were not less than 8 feet thick, but of their height no estimate can now he formed. The north-west angle of the square was slightly canted to suit the ground. Inside this enclosure was another square formed by walls of the same thickness as those just described, with a space between them of from 18 to 20 feet, and in this space the castle buildings have apparently stood. There are grass-covered traces of foundations against the north-east and south-east curtains, not, however, extending quite across the 18 feet space. At the inside angle of the north corner there has been a building of some kind about 20 feet square, with the walls seemingly brought up from a depth below the natural surface. This may have contained a well in the under-floor, or a tank or reservoir for water, such as are sometimes found in the earlier hill-forts.

The centre of the castle, which in ordinary cases would be called the court-yard, is here the natural sloping face of the hill-side, with several large rugged rocks projecting in confused masses through the ground. No attempt has been made to alter its surface by artificial means, but the space within the outer and inner walls (the 18 feet space) has been raised so as to be about level from north-east to south-west, with a fall to the north-east

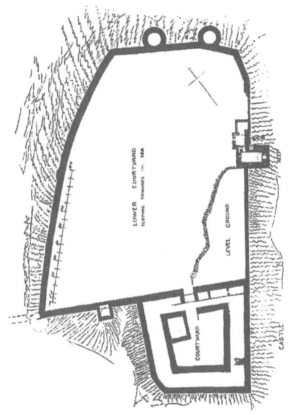

GROUND PLAN OF BRUCE'S CASTLE.

corner. The making-up, as seen on the north-east side, has been on an average about 6 feet, but considerably more along the north-west, owing to the fall of the hill being in this direction.

Great Court-yard and Towers

Adjoining the castle to the north-east there is a second and larger enclosure, already referred to as being the work of Bruce. This forms the lower court, which, like the court of the castle just described, is the rugged, rocky, unaltered surface of the hill-side. This court measures about 300 feet by 240 feet. Two of its sides are formed by a continuation of two sides of the castle proper. At the east corner the wall bends inwards to meet the north-east wall, which is strengthened by two drum towers about 28 feet in diameter and 40 feet apart. These towers defend the approach to the castle by the sea, and probably the entrance gate-way was situated at the bend of the wall near this point. The north-west enceinte is a continuous crescent-shaped wall, shown on the Ordnance Plan, as having had a drum-tower at its junction with the south-west wall (shown by dotted lines) but of this there is now no trace. On the latter wall, about 30 feet distant from the castle, are the remains of a square mural tower, measuring about 20 feet each way. This wall seems to have been continued down to the sea, but extensive quarrying operations on a roadway with houses along the shore have obliterated its lower end. On the south-eastern wall stands the later keep and buildings

THE KEEP FROM THE S.W.

to be afterwards described. Of the north-east, south-west, and south-east walls just described there are considerable remains, and at their most ruinous parts they can be distinctly traced along their whole respective lengths. The north-east wall, with its drum-towers on the outside, is about 8 feet or 10 feet high. Of the crescent-shaped north-west wall nothing remains but its track along the brow of the hill.

At the southern corner of this court-yard, between the keep and the castle, is a triangular piece of ground about 135 feet long by 45 feet wide. It occupies the highest part of the court-yard, and is the only level ground within the walls, being made so artificially. It is about the same level as the first floor of the keep. The great court-yard above described has evidently been the basse-cour of the castle. Bruce found it necessary to add this to the original structure in order to make the castle conform to the plan then universally adopted. At the same time, he would appear (from the documentary evidence to be hereafter referred to) to have built a hall and a dwelling-house within the walls of the ancient fortress, thus converting the whole into a genuine castle of the thirteenth century type.

The keep already referred to is of late fifteenth or early sixteenth century work, and stands near the centre of the south-east wall of the lower court-yard. It measures 41 feet by 26 feet 3 inches over, and is four stories in height. Up till nearly the middle of this century [nineteenth] its four walls were entire, with stairs leading to the various floors, continued round the north, west, and south walls in the thickness of the walls (as at Hallbar, Coxton, etc,), but about that time nearly all the south-west and south-east walls fell. The keep is now the only portion of Tarbert Castle, which bulks largely in the landscape, and it is doubtless owing to this that it has had conferred on it is the honour of being regarded as the castle

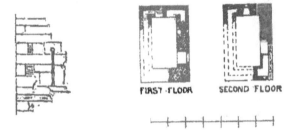

FIRST FLOOR   SECOND FLOOR

built by the great Bruce. The entrance at the north corner leads directly into the vaulted ground-floor, which is the only part now entire. It measures 26 feet by 12 feet 6 inches, and was, when clear of ruins, about 9 feet high.

At the south-east end is an arched recess in the wall, 4 feet 9 inches wide by 6 feet deep, having a broad splayed shot-hole for guns. This and a narrow splayed loop in the opposite wall supply all the lights on this floor. From the passage leading to the vault, the stair already mentioned leads off to the upper floors. There has been one apartment on each of these floors with wall chambers, and on the

CORBELLING

SLITS IN CLOSET 2ND FLOOR

top floor only is there a fireplace, but, doubtless, the two floors beneath contained fireplaces in the now fallen walls.

There   are   not   many   details   about   the   keep,   but   what   there are, as shown by sketches, all point to its erection at a late period. These are the gun-holes, several beaded windows, and beaded fire-place, parapet with its continuous corbelling, consisting of small members, and the general style of masonry.

Additions have been made to the keep on the north-east side, consisting of two apartments, probably two stories in height, and entering from the court-yard, with shot-holes on each side of the door. One of these apartments was probably the kitchen. There is a stone sink and drain in the north-east angle."

If now we turn to the statement of accounts furnished by the Constable of the Castle in the year 1326 we shall find many particulars bearing upon the extent of the operations undertaken by Bruce, as well as many interesting details of the cost of these operations, the rates of wages ruling at the period, and the cost of commodities. In addition to more or less expenditure upon the main building referred to above, the surrounding walls, and the outlying towers, we find that expense was incurred in the construction of a hall built on piers, houses within the inner court, with a middle wall enclosing it, and a chapel, together with such accessory structures as a *new* kitchen, a wine-house, bake-house, goldsmith's house, malthouse, brew-house, with *new* vat, a mill with millpond and lade, a moat, and a lime-kiln. The expenditure also includes "building a house in the isle anew, with roofing for the same," a part payment of £4 towards the building of a newe pele (fort) at Wester Tarbert, and a sum of £8 to William Scott "as part payment of £13 6s. 8d., agreed for with him for making a road from the one Tarbert to the other," which is probably the road used at the present day.

From the record we learn that from the 18th day of April, 1325, to the 20th July of the following year, the whole amount of money received by the Constable for the building operations and other duties connected with his office was £518 13s. 8d. During the same period he had expended in all £511. For the expenses connected with some of the buildings, viz.: the houses within the inner court, the middle wall enclosing it, and the wine-house, the Constable had not had leisure to account, so they are not included in the expenditure of £511. Otherwise, we seem to have in this Roll what must be considered a tolerably complete statement of the outlay connected with the building operations, as well as of some other matters more or less intimately connected with the castle.

In passing it should be noted that at this date the current money of Scotland did not materially differ in value from that of the sister country, Scots money passing for its full value in England in the reign of Robert the Bruce, and down till about the year 1355. The depreciation of the currency in Scotland, which ultimately brought the pound Scots down in value to one-twelfth of the pound sterling belongs to a later age. During Bruce's reign the pound weight of silver was coined into 26s. 3d.; at the present day the same weight is made into 66s.

As was to have been expected, the great bulk of the expenditure was on mason work. To Robert, the principal contractor for the mason work, a sum of £282 15s. was paid, besides a gratuity of £5 6s. 8d., "because, in the king's absence, he had built the walls wider than agreed on." John, another mason, received £28 7s. 8d., "by bargain for building the said castle;" while Adam, a third mason, was paid "by covenant for building the said castle £9 10s.;" and a further sum of £50 "for burning seven hundred and sixty chalders of lime for that building." The roofing of the "houses in the castle" occupied two roofers for forty days, and for this large undertaking their wages amounted to 13s. 4d., just 2d. per day for each man.

Of the skilled workmen, whose wages are specified, the best paid was Neil, the smith, who received 9d. per day. Next to him came Neil, the plumber, with 8d. per day; while John, the carpenter, got 6d. a day. Compared with these the stipend of the chaplain—Sir Maurice by name—can hardly he considered satisfactory, for it is put down at the modest sum of £2 for the half-year. Indeed, when we find that even the Constable, the chief officer of the castle, received no more than 1s. a day, it is highly probable that the skilled workman who received 8d. or 9d. a day was very well off with his seemingly insignificant wage.

Several items of expenditure, other than payments to contractors and workmen, are of very considerable interest. Sixteen chalders of coal, equal to twenty-four tons, were used for "the work done by Patrick the smith," and cost £1 1s. 4d. Five horses "for the carriage of lime" were purchased for £1 17s. The expense of bringing four of them from Islay was but 10s 6d., including 6d. which the man who had gone for them received as his wage.

The king appears to have taken a very keen interest in the building of the castle and the other work in connection with it. He

FROM THE "NEW QUAY."

visited it in 1325, when it would seem some of the contracts were entered into. The following year, accompanied by his warm friends, Lamberton, Bishop of St. Andrews and Primate of Scotland, and the Good Lord Douglas, names well-known and loved by all Scotsmen, he resided in it for some time. He had probably in his train also the Lords Auditors of the Exchequer, for we learn that during this visit, "he received the accounts of several of the local stewards." In those days the officers who collected the king's revenues rendered their accounts yearly before the Lords Auditors, receiving due notice to attend at a given time and place. On such occasions the Lords usually sat from four to six weeks, changing their place of sitting if the king shifted his residence during that period.

In connection with this latter visit, it is noted that James Del More received the sum of £2 1s. "to make provision at Tarbert for the king's need," while at the same time there was delivered to "John, clerk of the kitchen," twelve codri of cheese valued at 12s. In preparation for the other guests, a sum of 2s. 2½d. was expended in providing "litter for the chambers of the Lord Bishop of St. Andrews and Sir James. Lord of Douglas, with the cutting and carriage of branches of birch for repairing the hall and chambers." "Keeping forty of the queen's sheep before the arrival of the king" cost 1s.; "keeping the poultry for fifteen days," 1s. 10½d.; "keeping the king's mart and swine by two shepherds and two lads," seven bolls of meal; "watching bran for the dogs at Wester Tarbert for three weeks," 2s. 6d. Ample provision was evidently made "for the king's need," and it is reasonable to infer from some of the items that he was a frequent visitor, and while there enjoyed the pleasures of the chase. "Copin Wef, the merchant, by the king's order for clothes bought of him at Tarbert" received £1 6s. 8d.; "carriage of bread from Tarbert to Skipness," cost 1s. 10d.; "driving marts to Skipness twice," 8d.; "keeping and watching a prisoner," 3s. 4d.; and "one hundred large boards bought and send to Cardross for repairing the park," 3s. 4d.

From these records out of which the above particulars have been gleaned, a full statement may be gathered of the sources from which the funds for the buildings, etc., were obtained. At that period wages were largely paid in provisions, such as oatmeal and cheese. These, indeed, constituted the staple of the dietary of the people; and, when they were taken as part wages, the allowance given to a man for a month was generally one boll of meal and one codrus (about a stone) of cheese. From numerous entries in the accounts, it is evident that the chief source from which these commodities were obtained was Islay, and they were supplied in such quantities that large consignments were made to the king at Cardross, and to the chamberlain, "Sir Robert of Peblis."

By far the greater part of the cost was met by the gentlemen in authority all around the west coast. Dugald Campbell, Sheriff of Argyll (or Ergadia, as it was then written), and Bailie of Athole, is credited with contributing a considerable portion, while a larger amount in the shape of oatmeal and cheese was forwarded by John M'Donald, Bailie of Islay. Contributions were also sent in by "Dofnald, Neil, and John M'Gil-hon"—the last of them the ancestor of the M'Leans of Duart, and by "Gilchrist M'Ay," the progenitor of the M'Kays of Ugadale, the Bishop of Sodor, the Rector of Arran, the Abbot of Paisley, the Bailie of Kintyre, and others.

In the records of the year 1329 acknowledgment is made of £7, having been received by De Lany "out of the farms of Buchan, for the work of Tarbert," and of a sum of £2 from William of Bonkill (near Milngavie). A payment of £2 was also made in the same year to William Scott for "making and maintaining the park of Tarbert," and a further sum of £5 to the same individual in 1330 as allowance in full for the said park. In all probability this park was the lower courtyard. Such an appendage to the castle was very necessary, in view of the horses, cattle, sheep, and poultry, which, as we have seen from payments made, were kept in the neighbourhood.

YACHTING IN SUMMER SEAS.

No attempt, so far as we know, has been made to determine the site of the hall built on piers, the malt-house, the brew-house, the mill with its mill-pond and lade, and the moat. From the configuration of the ground the moat must necessarily have been limited to the south-east and the south-west sides. The appearance of the ground makes it probable that on the latter side the cut was situated about 100 yards south-west of the old castle. There are no similar surface indications on the low ground bounding the south-east, but the moat, doubtless, ran along that side also.

Nor has the site of the "pele" or fort at West

Tarbert been localised. No remains of such a structure exist, nor of another which is traditionally associated with the middle of the isthmus. Tarbert Castle and these fortified strengths formed part of a chain of forts extending along the western side of Kintyre, and communicating with one another by means of beacon fires. On the east Tarbert Castle in turn flashed the signal to forts on the Cowal shore, and these to Skipness, thence to Lochranza and the Ayrshire coast, and thus the approach of an enemy was heralded.

> "Is yon red glare the western star?—
> Oh, 'tis the beacon-blaze of war!
> .   .   .   .
> Each after each they glanced to sight,
> As stars arise upon the night."

It is said, and with considerable probability, that Robert Stewart, who afterwards became King Robert II., was the first upon whom the office of Keeper of Tarbert Castle was bestowed by Bruce. T. P. White, in his "Archæological Sketches in Kintyre," asserts that to a member of the Clan Campbell was first committed the important charge. However that may be, we certainly know that, conscious of the enormous power that had been about this time placed in the hands of the Mac Donalds by the gift of the king, the latter took the precautionary measure of obtaining from Angus Oig the resignation of his lands in Kintyre. These Bruce bestowed upon Robert Stewart, who was the son and heir of Walter the High Steward, and his wife the Princess Marjory Bruce.

Whether or not after the year 1326 the king again visited Tarbert we have no certain information. Two entries in which it is stated that wine and salt were bought "by the king at Tarbert" in 1329, may warrant the inference that he was resident in the castle in this year. Two other items in the accounts of the same year may point also in this direction. They refer to the "king's great ship." The first is one of 18s. paid to twelve men passing from Dumbarton to Tarbert "to bring back the great ship belonging to the king." The other is a note of six shillings paid to twelve men "passing with John, the son of Gun, to Tarbert, with the rigging of the king's great ship." The inference is further strengthened by the fact of a Court jester having been brought to Tarbert in 1329. The entry bearing upon it states that eighteenpence was paid "for the expenses of the men who accompanied Patrick the fool from England to Tarbert." Though a man of war the king enjoyed relaxation when the opportunity offered. In 1315, after he had subdued the Islesmen, he dwelt among them for a time, as Barbour tells us, enjoying himself to the full:—

> "All that sesoun thar duellyt he,
> At huntyng. gamyn, and at gle."

He had doubtless his high times at Tarbert also!

HOMEWARD BOUND.

Tarbert, a Royal Burgh.

For a period extending over many centuries, Tarbert was in certain respects the most important place in the county of Argyle, a fact due to its central geographical position. It appears in history as a Royal Burgh as far back as the year 1328. How much earlier it was possessed of these privileges it is impossible to state, but it is, in any case, the oldest Royal Burgh in the shire. According to Bell's "Law of Scotland," royal burghs, as a rule, sprung up beside royal castles; and, in the preface to vol. I. of the Exchequer Rolls, it is stated that this would seem to have been the case with regard to Tarbert.

In the year above-mentioned, a charge of seven shillings and eightpence is made by Sir Robert of

Peblis, Chamberlain of Scotland, for "making a coket for the burgh of Tarbert." The use of this coket or cocket-seal will be understood by a reference to the following extract from the preface above-mentioned: –

"Merchandise liable to custom could not be legally exported without a cocket, that is a certificate under the seal of the proper officer, that the great custom had been paid on it; and every burgh of export had its cocket seal and cocket clerk. One of the items of expenditure in the Chamberlain's account of 1328 is the making of a cocket for the burgh of Tarbert. . . . When goods were shipped

OUT FROM THE HARBOUR.

at one port under the cocket of another, they were included in the articles charged for, but the cocket appeared on the credit side of the account; and we find the custumars of Berwick, Edinburgh, Aberdeen, and Perth, crediting themselves on various occasions with cockets not only of the royal burghs of Linlithgow, Inverkeithing, Stirling, Cupar, and Tarbert, but of the Earl of Moray's burgh of Lochmaben, and of the church burgh of Dunfermline. . . .

"The custumars were persons appointed by the Crown in each burgh of export, being generally one or two of the leading burgesses, to collect the king's great custom."

In this extract, Tarbert, it will be observed, is classed as one of the royal burghs. In those early days such burghs were specially called upon to tax themselves for the support of the country, and in the year 1329 Tarbert is credited with the sum of £4 8s. 10d. as the "contributio pacis" of the burgh. This appears to have been a contribution towards the amount which was paid by Scotland to England as a war indemnity in terms of the treaty of Northampton.

As the gateway, more particularly in winter, to and from the Western Isles, Tarbert must have been from the earliest times a considerable centre of export, and its status as a royal burgh would add to its importance in this respect. The following extract from a "Report on the Settlement of the Revenues of Excise and Customs in Scotland" bears upon this in an interesting manner. The Report was submitted in 1656 to Cromwell's Government by a Mr Thomas Tucker. From the geographical discrepancies, it is very evident that Mr Tucker had not visited the district with which he deals. There can be no doubt, however, that the reference is to Tarbert. It is of special interest to us as showing the position occupied by Tarbert in the seventeenth century as a place of export, as well as from the fact that it gives an indication of the class of merchandise which the Highlanders of that time brought to market. The extract runs as follows:—

The inhabitants of Glasgow trade and deal "with their neighbours, the Highlanders, who come hither from the Isles and westerne parts; in summer by the Mul of Cantyre, and in winter by the Torban to the head [should rather be the mouth] of Loquh Fyn (which is a small neck of sandy land, over which they usually draive their small boats into the Firth of Dunbarton), and so passe up in the Cluyde with pladding, dry hides, goate, kid and deer skyns, which they sell, and purchase with theyr price such comodityes and provisions as they stand in neede of from time to time."

The quotation is also of interest as showing that in times of peace as well as in the affairs of war, it was customary for the travellers to drive or drag their boats across the isthmus. The practice is referred to by George Buchanan in his history written in 1582:— "Kintyre is joined to Knapdale by an isthmus of sand, scarcely a mile across, so low that the sailors often drag their vessels over it in order to shorten their navigation." Pennant, who wrote his "Tour" in 1772, may also be quoted in the same connection:— "It is not very long since vessels of nine or ten tuns were drawn by horses out of the west loch into that of the east to avoid the dangers of the Mull of Cantyre, so dreaded and so little known was the navigation round that promontary." In the continued absence of a ship canal or a ship railway the same practice is still pursued, though to a more limited extent since the formation of the Crinan Canal.

The report of Tucker, quoted above, finds an interesting echo in quite modern times, in a reference to the same practice made by Lord Teignmouth, who, in 1827, passed by the Tarbert route to the Western Isles at a time when the Crinan Canal was closed for repairs. In his "Sketches," to which I shall refer later, he writes:—"It was the ancient practice to drag vessels of small size across the isthmus . . . and since the recent closing of the Crinan Canal it has been resumed by the fishermen of Barra and other islands, who, rather than trust their commissions to strangers, persevere in a custom now gradually growing into disuse, of carrying the fish which they catch to the Clyde markets, and purchase the little luxuries and articles of dress which their slender profits command."

TRANSPORTING IN MODERN FASHION.

Land ownership in the neighbourhood in early times.

Among the many changes of ownership which the lands in the neighbourhood of Tarbert had undergone from one cause or other before the beginning of the sixteenth century, it is difficult to trace the proprietorship connectedly. In the thirteenth century, and for some centuries later, Tarbert, and much of the north of Kintyre, formed part of the barony or lordship of Knapdale. Early in the thirteenth century most of Knapdale, including the lands of Skipness and those in the neighbourhood of Clachan, seem to have been possessed by Syfyn or Swene of Argyll. As early as 1262, Dufgal, the son of Swene, granted to Walter Steward, "Earl of Menthet," his land of Skipness reaching over the county to Clachan, "in free barony for payment to the King of two-thirds of the service of one soldier and other services." At some time previous to the year 1310, Robert Bruce is said to have granted Knapdale to John of Menthet, a descendant of the above Walter Steward; but in this year "King Edward II. of England, in order that John, the son of Swien of Argyll, and Terrealnanogh and Murquocgh, his brothers, might render themselves more hateful to John of Meneteth, his enemy, and to others his enemies in Scotland, granted to them the whole land of Knapdale which belonged to their ancestors, provided they could recover it out of his enemies' hands." In this extract we have an interesting illustration of one of the methods employed by the English for increasing their influence and furthering their ends in these remote districts.

Similarly, in the year 1335, Edward Baliol, when his star was for the moment in the ascendant, granted to John, Lord of the Isles, who "favoured the English interest," "Mull, Skye, Islay, and Gigha, as well as Kintyre and Knapdale." This coquetting of the son of the loyal Angus Oig with Baliol was viewed with great concern by the Scottish Government, and negotiations were entered into with John of the Isles. In order the more expeditiously and conveniently to carry out these negotiations, John, Earl of Moray, the guardian of Scotland, resided within the castle of Tarbert for a considerable portion of the time during which they were in progress. Before they were completed, he was called south to repel an invasion of French troops who had come to assist the English.

Forty-one years later—1376—"King Robert II, granted to John Del Yle [of the Isles], and Margaret, his wife, half of his lands in Knapdale."

"In 1475, John, Earl of Ross, and Lord of the Isles forfeited all his possessions to the crown, and, on his restoration in 1476, the lordship of Knapdale was reserved to the crown."

In 1481, King James III. seems to have restored to the MacDonalds all the more modern lordship of Knapdale, which, however, it is noted, was claimed by "Makelane and Maknele." In this grant, the place names of the district included are all given, and most of them are easily recognisable in their somewhat archaic spelling.

MANŒUVRING FOR THE START.

Royal Visits and the Building of the Keep.

After the final forfeiture of the Lordship of the Isles in 1493, James IV., with characteristic activity, busied himself in securing the submission of the vassals of the lordship, and in consolidating his kingdom in the north and west. That same year he visited Campbeltown. The following year he resided on two occasions at Tarbert. During his first visit, which occurred in April, "he repaired," says Tytler, "the fort originally built by Bruce, and established an emporium for his shipping, transporting thither his artillery, laying in a stock of gunpowder, and carrying along with him his master gunners, in whose training and practice he appears, from the payments in the treasurer's books, to have busied himself with much perseverance and enthusiasm."

King James IV. at Tarbert

The second visit was made in July. That occasion is rendered somewhat memorable by the fact that Parliament was summoned to meet him there in order to deliberate on the means to be employed for securing a more settled state of affairs in Kintyre and the Southern Isles. The reference to this visit in the preface to Vol. I. of the accounts of the Lord High Treasurer states that "on the 5th of July, 1494, the lords of the east, south, and west, were summoned to meet King James IV. at Tarbert, where, accordingly, we find him on the twenty-fourth with the *Christopher* and other ships, gunners and munitions of war. Having repaired the castle of Tarbert, and victualled and garrisoned it as a basis of operations, he proceeded to reduce the castle of Dunaverty, in South Kintyre."

The expenses connected with the summoning of the Lords at this time, and the method by which it was effected, are gathered from the two following entries in the treasurer's accounts:—"In primis the V. day of Julii, gevin to Donald Malynne, currour, to pass with letters to the Lords of the Westland for the meeting of the King at the Terbert, xs." "Item to John Keir to pass with sic lik letters in the Southland and the Eastland, xiiii."

Still another courier is sent, in the same connection, from Glasgow, with writings to his Majesty.

As illustrating the King's generosity and the habits of the times, the following entry is interesting and significant:—"Item gevin to the gunnaris, the xxiiii. day of Julii, be the King's command, to drink-silver, xls." The gift was evidently bestowed on the arrival of the ships at Tarbert.

Nor were the necessities of the chapel overlooked, for mention is made of a sum of £6 13s. 4d. having been given towards its expenses "quhen the King was at the Terbert."

But the most interesting and important items in the accounts of 1494 are acknowledgments of sums received towards the "biggin of Tarbert." These probably point to the building of the Keep at this time, which, judged by its style of architecture, belongs, as has been shown, to this period. If this is so, the references to "repairs" upon the castle quoted above from Tytler and from the preface to the treasurer's accounts should rather be to the erection of this important addition to the castle buildings. The items are these:—"The Comptare charges him wyth xxli. ressauit frae the Bishop of Dunblane to the biggin of Tarbert," and a like sum was "resauit fra the Abbot of Newbotill for the said caus." In the same year, and probably for the same purpose, though it is not stated, there was delivered to "my Lord Chamberlain at the Tarbert," £66 13s. 4d.

The next occasion on which we find King James at Tarbert was in the year 1498. This journey to the west is thus referred to in the preface already quoted:—"He sailed on the 8th of March [from Ayr], and, touching at Arran, proceeded to the new castle which he

MADA-BUIDHE.

had built at the head of Loch Kilkerane, now Campbeltown, in South Kintyre. Having spent a week there and at Tarbert, he returned by way of Ayr to Duchal." "Desirous of providing for the strongholds he had established there and at Tarbert, he sometime after sent 'ane cole man to pas in Kintyre to vesy gif colis may be wonnyne thare.'" Following this entry in the accounts is one of eighteen shillings paid to a Dumbarton collier to make working tools and proceed into Kintyre.

In April, 1499, we find this able and energetic monarch once more at Tarbert, bent on the pacification of rival clans. About this time a new policy began to be adopted for the enforcement of order in the more seriously disturbed districts, and in the course of this year we find the Government applying it to the districts around Tarbert. This policy consisted in the giving of grants to some of the more powerful nobles, and vesting them with authority, and the duty of maintaining order in those particular districts in which they were given a proprietary interest. During the visit of the King at this time, large favours were conferred upon the Clan Campbell, who had always been loyal to the throne. Upon Argyll was bestowed "a commission of Lieutenandry, with the fullest powers, over the Lordship of the Isles." A few months later, he "was appointed Keeper of the Castle of Tarbert, and Bailie and Governor of the King's lands in Knapdale."

The Barony of Tarbert.

But these concessions were only the beginning of good things in this neighbourhood for the house of Argyll. In 1505, there was "granted to the same earl the offices of Justiciar and Chamberlain of the lands and lordships of Knapdaill and Kintyre, and of Captain of the house and fortalice of Tarbert, and also the lands of Kilberry and the south half of Knapdaill, with the patronage of the church of Kilberry (all united into the barony of Tarbert), with one half of the King's dues." In the years 1526, 1529, 1540, 1541, and 1542, the grants in one form or other were renewed and confirmed, and the keeping of the castle of Tarbert has ever since remained in the hands of the family of MacCalein Mor as the feudal superiors.

A Pirate 'mid the Hebrides.

In the disturbed social conditions which existed at this time, men of predatory tendencies with the necessary daring and initiative, found full play on sea not less than upon land for the furtherance of individual ambition. One of the most successful and most noted of those piratical marauders who swept the western seas in the early years of the sixteenth century was Alan-nansop, who died about the year 1555. Allan was an illegitimate son of Lachlan Catanach MacLean of Duart, chief of the Clan MacLean, by a daughter of the laird of Treshinish. How he came to get his nickname of Alan-nan-sop (Alan of the straw) is uncertain. According to one story it arose from his having been born, by some accident, on a heap of straw, while according to another it came to him in consequence of a custom which was specially his of setting fire to houses by means of a blazing wisp of straw when on his freebooting expeditions. In any case, no Highlander need long be without a nickname!

Some years after the birth of Alan, the beauty of his mother having captivated MacLean of Torloisk, he married her, and took her to reside at his castle of Torloisk.

Unfortunately for Alan, and still more for the young man's future victims, he drew upon himself, in some way or other, the ill-will of his step-father. Alan was therefore forced to shift for himself, and to strive by foul means, if not by fair, to win an inheritance independently of the old chieftain. Young, strong, and brave to desperation, he joined himself to one of the numerous ships engaged in piracy along the coast, and "in process of time obtained the command, first of one galley, then of a small flotilla, with which he sailed round the seas and collected considerable plunder, until his name became both feared and famous."

This picturesque rover is of interest to us, for he resided for a time in the Castle of Tarbert, and had considerable possessions in the neighbourhood. In the Gaelic magazine, "Cuairtear Nan Gleann," of August, 1841, an interesting paper may be found upon Alan, which the writer says is an earnest attempt to give a true and faithful account of the doings of his hero. Others, to the writer's regret, had circulated many untruths regarding him. Here we give a translation of that part of the paper which refers more particularly to Tarbert. Regarding the gift of Tarbert Castle, which it is there said was bestowed upon Alan by MacDonald of Islay, we may suppose he received it from the latter for the taking of it from his hereditary enemies the Campbells. Once in his possession, Argyll evidently preferred to have him as a friend rather than as a foe.

"There is nothing," says this writer, "which shows more plainly the cunning and might of this man than the fact that MacDonald of Islay bought his friendship by giving him as an estate the island of Gigha and villages at the head of Loch Tarbert. This warrior or robber spent much time in the Castle of Tarbert, which he obtained from MacDonald; and M'Cailein Mor bought his friendship by giving him an estate in Knapdale, a fertile region called Kilcharmaig.

"By the friendship of these great men, MacCailein, MacDonald, and his brother, Hector Mor of Duart, Ailean-nan-Sop was exceedingly powerful, and became a cause of terror to his enemies; but, although he possessed so many valuable estates, he did not cease plundering and destroying. From Tarbert Castle he used to go to Cowal and to Loch Lomond side, and through the country of the Lowlands,

"CORINTHIANS" ARRIVING.

carrying off booty from every place. He used also to go with ships to Ireland, burning and destroying and carrying off plunder, so that Ailean-nan-Sop was as well known in Ireland as he was in Scotland. He went once to collect spoil from the Isle of Bute; the sheriff heard that he was coming, and gathered his men, but they could not withstand the bold warriors who were with Alan; he brought away a shipful of cattle, the best that he could get.

"Alan's conduct caused great sorrow to that high-minded and honourable man, Hector Mor, his brother, and to his kinsman, the Lord of Coll. Alan heard something that the Lord of Coll had said against him, and he set off to Coll to take vengeance on him. The Lord of Coll was walking on the shore; Alan laid hold of him and took him on board his boat, made him prisoner, and tied him to a rower's bench, hoisted his sail, and set off to Tarbert.

"The Lord of Coll was a noted bard, and he began to make a song to Ailean-nan-Sop. He sang the song—this got the better of Alan—he loosed him and gave him his freedom, saying to him. 'Take care what you say about me after this— there is a little bird in Coll that comes to tell me your language at your own table— I will let you go, but be on your guard henceforth.'

"When Alan became old, he gave up his evil habits and abandoned plundering and robbing, but this did not please his warriors who were in the castle—the flesh was not so plentiful as it used to be. On a certain day he gave a feast, and one of his men was picking a bone on which there was not much to be got. 'A wonderful change has come on this house,' said he, 'when the bones are so bare.' Alan heard him, and understood what was meant—'Let every boat that belongs to us be ready to-night, our boys and our men, and we will try to put in a little flesh for the winter.' Off they set through the Kyles of Bute, and went up the river Clyde to near Glasgow; they took much spoil, and returned with every boat filled. This is the greatest and the last booty that Ailean-nan-Sop ever took, and he gave it the name of the 'spoil of the rib' (in allusion to the bone which his follower had been picking).

"Alan became very aged. He went to Icolmkill and made his peace with the clergy, and shortly afterwards died and was buried in Iona in St. Oran's burying ground with his ancestors, the family of Duart.

"Alan had one son and one daughter. He put his son to death because he attempted to murder Hector Mor, his father's brother; and his daughter married Murdoch the Short, of Lochbuy. The estate that Alan took from the 'Family of the Iron Sword,' the family of Leitir, came after his death to MacLean of Duart, and he gave it to Lachlan Og, son of Sir Lachlan Mor of Duart, and from him came the family of Torloisk.

"Ailean-nan-Sop   died   about   the   year   1555   —   between that and 1560. The flat stone on this man's grave can be discovered in Icolmkill. "

HARVESTING AT CARNBAN.

The Sheriffdom of Tarbert.

Clan strifes, bloody and frequent, creachs on land, and piracies by sea, made the administration of law in the Highlands and Islands an undertaking of the greatest difficulty. Within Argyll and its many islands the task was, for centuries, almost an impossible one. From time to time the organisation of the district was strengthened, but always with results disappointing to those who had the good government of the country at heart. In the fifteenth century, to facilitate administration, the northern portions of the shire were attached to Inverness, the central and larger portion of the mainland constituted the sheriffdom of Lorne or Argyll, and the remainder was formed into the shire or sheriffdom of Tarbert. The existence of the shire of Tarbert may be traced as far back as the year 1481, but the date of formation cannot be arrived at.

Its extent was very considerable, for it included within its jurisdiction the districts of Kintyre and

Knapdale, together with the islands of Gigba, Islay, Jura, Scarba, Colonsay, Mull, and a number of the smaller isles. With our present want of knowledge of the determining circumstances, it seems to us somewhat of an anomaly when we find that previous to 26th February, 1481, when it was made a part of the shire of Tarbert, the district of Knapdale was included in the shire of Perth. At an earlier period still, however, it formed a portion of the shire of Lorne or Argyll.

But even this organisation was not sufficient to meet the necessities of the case. In the year 1503, deputy sheriffs were appointed for the north Isles and for "the south Ilis and thai partis" to further aid in the administration of justice. The Act is very illuminating and instructive, as it pictures the necessity for these appointments:—"Item becaus thair hes bene greit abusioun of Justice in the northt partis and west partis of the realme, sic as the northt Ilis and south Ilis, for lak and falt of Justiceairis Justicis, and schirefis And thairthrou the pepill ar almaist gane wild It is thairfor statute and ordainit for the acquietting of the pepill be Justice that thair be in tyme to cum Justicis and schirefs depute in thai partis as eftir folowis that is to say That the Justicis and schirefs of the northt Ilis haif thair sait and place for administratioun of Justice in Inverness or Dingwale as the materis occurris to be decernyt be the saidis officiaris And that ane uther Justice and schiref be maid and depute for the south Ilis and thai partis and to haif his place and sait for administratioun of Justice in the tarbart or at lochkinkerane at the will and plesour of the saidis officiaris as the materis occurris."

As the seat of a Sheriff, Tarbert would, doubtless, during those troublous times, witness many a stirring scene, when, at its "mercatt croce or accustomat place," citations and "summonds" were issued against offenders, denunciations of hornings against recalcitrants, and proclamations against the Clan Ian or other restless tribe.

Where was that market cross, and where the Sheriff's seat and court-house? Popular tradition has always associated with the court-house an old thatched cottage, which, until twelve years ago, had flanked the eastern end of the back street. Its site is now occupied by the handsome church erected shortly before the Union by the Free Church. Whether or not the old cottage was the original court-house, it is probable that the site it occupied is correctly associated with the old seat of justice. The situation indicated would in early times be the most central spot in the village, and we may take it that close by the court-house would be the "mercatt croce" or "accustomat place."

Until its demolition, this old cottage communicated with an adjoining house by means of an underground vault. It is unlikely that this vault was in existence when law reigned supreme within the walls of the cottage, for it does not seem to have been intended to serve any more noble purpose than the ends of illicit distilling. This favourite occupation of the Highlander appears to have been extensively carried on within it, and the usual difficulty with regard to the smoke is understood to have been overcome by introducing it into the chimney of the courthouse.

FROM THE BASE OF MAOLDARACH.

Some of the most stirring events of the time found an echo around that old "mercatt croce." Proclamations as to the holding of wappinschaws and the assembling of military levies for service often filled the air in those troublous times. "Forasmekle as it is maist requisite that in time of peace provision be maid and cair taken for the weare when at goddis pleasur it may happen," it was enacted on 5th March, 1574, that "wappinschawis" should be held twice a year—on July 20th and October 10th—at convenient places within the several jurisdictions. In order that the Government might have a thorough and complete knowledge of the military capabilities of each district, our prudent forefathers arranged that these gatherings should be held on the same day all over the country, and James Campbell, of Ardkinglas, and Dugald Campbell, of Auchinbreck, were commissioned at this time to co-operate with the Sheriff and the other officials of the shire of Tarbert in receiving the musters, and examining the arms, armour, etc. Within forty days after the wappinschaw, the Sheriffs and Bailies forwarded to the Regent, under a penalty of one hundred marks, a complete list of the muster and of the weapons, and thus the Government was kept fully informed of the country's state of preparedness for war.

Probably as the result of those field days and the increased control thus gained over the clans, levies from such outlying districts as the shire of Tarbert came to be more frequently employed for Imperial purposes in other and distant parts of the country. In the year 1579 a levy of all the inhabitants within the shire of Tarbert was ordered for service at the siege of the castles of Hamilton and Draffen, held by the Hamiltons against the King. In 1580, 1582 and 1588, levies were raised for employment against the Border thieves; in 1584, against the "enemies of the true religion in the North"; in 1592 and 1601, against the MacGregors; and in 1596 and 1608 against the Islesmen.

In the year 1597, those men of the shire of Tarbert were for the fourth time called upon for service against the Border thieves. On this occasion, however, they were allowed to compromise in the matter of numbers. The proclamation is interesting, inasmuch as it details the arms and armour which the "hundreth hieland men" were to provide themselves with. It shall be lawful, says the proclamation, to the "haill inhabitants of Tarbett, comprehending thairin Ergyll," to furnish "ane hundreth hieland men with a commander bodin with hacquetbutis, bowis, havirshonis, swerdis, darlochis and targeis," and the observance of this alternative by the sheriffdom "sall releve the haill remanent inhabitants thairof fra thair personal service to this present raid." Those were the days of transition, when the musket was still supplemented by the bow, and the body was protected by habergeon and target.

Until its amalgamation (when peace was more assured) with the shire of Argyll, the shire of Tarbert returned its member to the Scottish Parliament from time to time. Its last representative was Sir Lachlan M'Lean of Morvern, who had been elected by the freeholders in September, 1628. The hereditary offices connected with the shire were, for the greater part of its existence, held by the house of Argyll. Among these offices were those of Heritable Lieutenant, Chamberlain, Sheriff, and Coroner.

APPROACHING THE PIER.

The shire of Tarbert was abolished in the year 1633, in accordance with an Act of Parliament passed on 28th June of that year. Its abolition was in these terms following; —"His Majestie with advyse and consent of the thrie estates of this present Parliament, Hes united and be thir presents unites The said shirefdome of Tarbett to the forsaid shirefdome of Argyll, And ordaines baith the saidis shirefdoms of Argyll and Tarbett heirby united as said is To be callit in all tyme coming the shirefdome of Argyll." Further, "no citations, sumonds, denunciationes of hornings, inhibitiones, brieves, nor na uther sick publick citations or proclamationes sall be usit at na tyme heireftir at the mercatt croce or accustomat place of Tarbett." And thus passed the shire of Tarbert, whose institution and continuance marked a troublous period in the history of the Argyllshire seaboard and the Western Isles. It is to be noted, however, that for many years after 1633 the phrase "Shire of Tarbert" continued to be used in proclamations, letters, etc., showing that for practical purposes, such as the massing of levies, the subdivision was felt to be very convenient. Not till the year 1705 do we find the expression "Tarbet in the shire of Argyll" occurring in the records.

A Project of King James VI.

The sixteenth century had almost run its course, but not yet had those more peaceful times dawned in the west to which we have just referred; and in the year 1600 the tide of war threatened to surge once again across the isthmus. James VI. was, for the moment, in one of his courageous moods, and in order to bring his rebellious subjects to subjection, he formed the brave resolve to undertake an expedition in person to Kintyre and the Isles. Accordingly a proclamation was issued in April, 1600, commanding the inhabitants of the shires of Ayr, Renfrew, Dumbarton, and several other districts, to meet him at Dumbarton on the 10th of July. Two days after this date he hoped to reach Tarbert, where all within the bounds of Tarbert, Bute, Argyll, Athole, and Breadalbane were instructed to await his arrival. To the "ferry of Tarbett" all the boatmen and ferriers upon the water of Clyde, and the whole sea-coast thereabout were summoned to repair with their boats upon the said 12th July, there to attend for transporting the army, under pain of loss of life, lands and goods.

It was, indeed, a "brave resolve." In imagination we see the castle once again tenanted by a king. We look upon a scene full of bustle and stir as the galleys are drawn across to the Western Loch; and our ears ring with the shouts of the soldiery as they march over the isthmus under their royal leader. At the last moment, however, the expedition was abandoned, firstly, on account of the poverty and distress of the people of Scotland at that time, and secondly, for what would probably appear to James the more important reason, viz.,—that he was afraid to "hasard himselff" among MacDonalds and MacLeans, MacNeils and MacKinnons, unless well supported by troops.

Such abortive attempts (and this was the third that had been contemplated within a very few years), were not calculated to induce respect for the central Government, and we need not wonder if Kintyre and the Southern Isles continued in a state of turbulence and strife. Highland blood was hot, and opportunities of quarrel were frequent; and Commissioners who visited Kintyre and the Isles from time to time with a view to effecting reconciliations and securing the personal submission of the chiefs, were usually frustrated in their efforts.

AWAITING SHIPMENT.

"Garrin' ane devil dang anither."

In Kintyre and the Southern Isles, the chief disturbing influence continued to be the MacDonalds and the several offshoots of that ancient and powerful clan. That their power should be curbed at all hazards seemed an absolute necessity to the Government, and no more convenient or less expensive method could be devised than that introduced in the fifteenth century of setting one powerful clan against another by holding out the inducement of increased territory. "Garrin' ane devil dang anither," was the expressive phrase usually employed to indicate such methods. Thus the opportunity of the Campbells again recurred, and early in the year 1607 Argyll succeeded in obtaining a grant of the lands in North and South Kintyre and in Jura, which had formerly belonged to Angus MacDonald.

Weakened by strife within the clan, and by the prolonged imprisonment of Sir James, their young chief, as well as by the frequent harassments of their enemies, the MacDonalds were not, for several years, in a position to effectively resent such wholesale deprivation of their ancestral possessions. In the spring of 1615, however, Sir James succeeded in effecting his escape from Edinburgh, and within a very short time was at the head of his clan with a following of four hundred men.

Feeling assured that an effort of a determined character would now be made by the MacDonalds to recover their territory and influence, Argyll was invested with the office of Lieutenant over Argyll, Tarbert, and the whole Western Isles, and was instructed so to proceed "that civil manners and customs might be established in these isles, and all their old barbarous customs utterly abolished."

Until the Earl's arrival from England, Sir Dugald Campbell of Auchinbreck was appointed to the chief command, and he was under orders to take measures for the protection of Argyll proper, Knapdale, and Kintyre. To his aid the militia of all the western shires were called out by proclamation.

By the end of July, Auchinbreck had gathered to him three hundred men, with whom he held the isthmus of Tarbert, his immediate object being the confining of the MacDonalds to Kintyre until the arrival of Argyll.

As was anticipated, Sir James MacDonald was not long inactive. Landing in Kintyre with a force of four hundred men, he hurried the fiery cross through the district, and toward the end of July moved northward in full force, taking up a position about ten miles from Tarbert. By the 30th of that month he hoped to reach the isthmus.

From some cause, however, which remains inexplicable, Sir James's activity was now arrested, and he made no effort to advance to the isthmus, and push his way out of the peninsula. This condition of inactivity continued until Argyll himself was actually in a position to attack him.

In the early days of September, the Earl, by means of spies, ascertained that Sir James MacDonald and about a thousand of his forces were encamped at Dunskeig, on the west coast of Kintyre, about ten miles from Tarbert, while a number of his galleys, under command of Coll, Keppoch, and others, rode at anchor in the neighbourhood of the island of Cara. To surprise these galleys by night, and seize them if possible, was the first aim of Argyll, and for that purpose he detached from the rendezvous in Loch Crinan a force of seven or eight hundred men under Sir John Campbell of Calder and other officers, while he himself took ship at Ardrishaig a few days later, and on the evening of the same day arrived at Tarbert with a force about equal in number to that of Calder. MacDougalls, Lamonts, and MacLachlans swelled the forces of the Earl, while there had also been

A CRITICAL SURVEY.

placed at his disposal by the Government four hundred hired soldiers.

It was now high time for Sir James to bestir himself. Hurrying forward his uncle Ranald with three or four hundred men to stop the passage from Tarbert on the east, he at the same time despatched Coll Ciotach from Cara with sixty men in three boats to reconnoitre at West Tarbert. There Coll succeeded

45

in capturing Colin Campbell of Kilberry and three or four of his followers, who were probably engaged on a similar duty on behalf of Argyll.

The southward march of the Earl, however, was the signal for the retreat of both Ranald and Coll; and Argyll steadily pursued his way in the direction of the camp of Sir James. By this time Calder and his forces had reached the island of Gigha, and, in his eagerness to verify the truth of a report to this effect which he had heard, Coll approached that isle so closely that he only escaped with difficulty. Finding his way to the coast of Kintyre, Coll forsook his boats and fled southward with all convenient speed, taking with him his prisoners. So hot, however, was the pursuit that fifteen or sixteen of his men were killed. Ere long he succeeded in reaching Islay. At this juncture Keppoch's rebel fleet at Cara, warned by beacons lit by some of Largie's men, loosed anchor and fled precipitately towards Kintyre, but they were closely followed by another part of Calder's fleet. Forsaking his ships on the Kintyre coast, Keppoch directed his steps towards the extreme south end of the peninsula.

This altered position of affairs, and the approach of the forces under Argyll, induced Sir James to immediately forsake his camp at Dunskeig, and seek safety in flight to Rathlin. Later on the unfortunate chief returned to Islay, then passed over to Ireland, and finally left the British Isles and sought a refuge in Spain. By the beginning of November the insurrection was completely quelled.

The year after the suppression of the rebellion (1616), Argyll, who was in great favour, obtained as a reward for his services, a grant of the Lordship of Kintyre, which was now alienated from the Crown, and settled upon James Campbell, a son of the Earl. Notwithstanding this transaction, however, both the Sanda branch and the Largie branch of the Clan Ian Mhor succeeded in preserving their estates from forfeiture. It was, nevertheless, a serious blow to the proud descendants of the mighty Somerled.

In 1619, when the Earl had gone abroad, after having become a Romanist, Campbell of Kilberry was required to answer for the peace of Kintyre, and among those who were called upon to assist him were MacAlister of Loup and MacAlister of Tarbert.

The Covenanting Army cross the Isthmus.

In the year 1647, eighteen months after the crushing defeat of the great Montrose at Philiphaugh, the only chief remaining in arms for the king in the south and west was Sir Alaster MacDonald of Dunaverty, son of Coll Ciotach, and the erstwhile Major-General of Montrose. At the date mentioned he was in Kintyre, which he so ravaged that in May General David Leslie and the Marquis of Argyll advanced with the Covenanting forces in order to expel him from the district. As illustrating the ease with which at that time it was felt the Isthmus

MAOLDARACH BAY AND OUTER HARBOUR.

of Tarbert might be held against any army endeavouring to enter Kintyre from the Knapdale side, the following letter may be quoted. It is from the pen of Sir James Turner, Adjutant-General of Leslie's army, and runs thus:—"From Inverary we marched to Kintyre, which is a peninsula. Both before, and at the entry to it, there were such advantages of ground that our foot, for mountains and marshes, could never have drawn up one hundred in a body, nor our horse above three in a breast, which, if Sir Alister had prepossessed with those thousand or twelve hundred brave foot which he had with him,

I think he might have ruined us—at least we should not have entered Kintyre (but by a miracle); but he was ordained for destruction, for, by a speedy march, we made ourselves masters of these difficult passes, and got into a plain country, where no sooner he saw our horse advance, but with little or no fighting, he retired." The fact seems to be that MacDonald, whose forces consisted of fourteen hundred foot and two troops of horse, was unaware of the approach of Leslie, and so the latter entered unopposed. The letter, however, illustrates afresh the strategical importance of Tarbert.

Tradition avers that the MacAlisters were at the moment busily engaged in an effort to take Skipness Castle from the Campbells, and that they failed to respond in time to Sir Alaster's instructions to defend the passes. When at last the siege was raised, they made a bold attempt, but without success, to arrest the advance at Mac-Munn's flagstone. Later, while Leslie awaited the approach of Argyll at Kintarbert, the MacAlisters marched south and joined Sir Alaster.

The result of the expedition, the defeat of Sir Alaster at Rhunahaorin, the capture of the castle of Dunaverty, and the brutal massacre of its garrison, are well known matters of Highland history.

Tarbert Castle in the time of the Commonwealth.

A little incident which occurred in the year 1652 serves to link Tarbert with the story of the times of the Commonwealth. During that period, Tarbert Castle, in common with most of the castles in Scotland, passed into the possession of the Roundheads, by whom it is stated to have been strengthened by the construction of bastions and outworks. According to Aikman's continuation of George Buchanan's history, it was thus recaptured by a body of Tarbert men. After referring to the fact that Argyll had been surprised by some Parliamentary forces while he lay ill at Inveraray, that he reluctantly submitted to the Commonwealth, that he accompanied their forces to Dumbarton, and that during his way thither some of his vassals, thinking or pretending to think, that he was a prisoner, stopped the march of the Roundheads through a certain defile, the historian proceeds thus:—"Others seized the castle of Tarbert on the same pretext during the absence of the greater part of the garrison, who had gone a-nutting, from which they took ten barrels of gunpowder, five thousand weight of cheese, and twenty-six bags of biscuit: for this, however, they afterwards made an apology to the major-general, who politically accepted it, and not being too rigid in requiring restitution, his forces were treated with more kindness in that district, and their officers entertained at the expense of Argyll, whose interests demanded that he should use them with hospitality, when further hostility would only have aggravated his irremediable ruin."

From a contemporary, Sir Bulstrode Whitelocke, we learn that the above incident occurred about the beginning of September, 1652, and that the officer who was in command of the garrison at the time

THREE JOLLY TARS.

of the surrender was Lieutenant Gillot. Speaking of the protection which had been afforded by Argyll to the forces of Colonel Overton in Kintyre and that neighbourhood, Balfour says:—"If my Lord Marquesse of Argyle had not protected him, he and all that wes with him had gottin ther throttes cutte. So, weill laughin at by the heighlanders, he wes forced to returne with penurey aneuche, werey glade all of them that ther lives were saved."

Eight years from the above date, the Commonwealth had ceased to be, Charles II. was restored to the throne whose privileges he had abused; the great Marquis of Argyll, to whom we have just referred, and who had placed the crown on the king's head at Scone, was speedily brought to the block, and some years afterwards his son, the Earl of Argyll, was condemned to death, but escaped into exile before the bloody deed could be committed. After the discovery of the Rye-house plot in England, measures were taken to prevent a rising in the Campbell country, it being asserted that the Earl had promised aid to the conspirators by calling his clansmen to arms against the Government in Scotland. These precautionary measures were of a very thorough nature, and over the shires of Argyle and Tarbert six lieutenants were placed, while a royal proclamation was issued on May 5th, 1684, commanding certain noblemen and gentlemen to hold in readiness a considerable force of armed men drawn from all parts of the country, these to come to the assistance of the lieutenants on six days' warning, and with thirty days' provision. Scotland remained undisturbed, however, at this time, and the preparations were unnecessary.

Argyll's Invasion of Scotland.

With the events of the following year, the history of Tarbert is intimately associated, and again the castle and the isthmus are thronged by armed men. The "Merry Monarch" had died, and the accession in February, 1685, of the Duke of York as James the Seventh of Scotland, and Second of England, brought no relief to the sorely persecuted covenanters, but rather enormously aggravated them.

Anticipating the great revolution that was at hand, English and Scottish exiles in Holland, weary of separation from their homes and disgusted with the grievous misgovernment of their country, resolved to raise the standard of rebellion both in England and Scotland.

The command of the Scottish expedition was conferred upon Archibald, Earl of Argyll. The significance of the appointment was not lost upon the king, as was made apparent by his remark to the Dutch ambassadors, when he said— "Of all men living, Argyll has the greatest means of annoying me." It being expected that the landing in Scotland would be effected in some part of the Earl's territory, active steps were taken to frustrate the attempt, even before the expedition had left the shores of Holland. The chief men of the Campbells were summoned to Edinburgh, where many of them were detained as hostages, and on the 29th of April, Argyll's enemy, the Marquis of Atholl, received a commission as Lord Lieutenant of the shires of Argyll and Tarbert. As a result of this appointment, eighteen gentlemen of the name of Campbell were executed at Inverary on a charge of rebellion and refusing to take the Test Oath.

On the second day of May, 1685, the expedition sailed from Holland. It consisted of three ships and about three hundred men, and accompanying the Earl were several influential covenanters, the most prominent being Sir Patrick Hume and Sir John Cochrane.

Arrived at Dunstaffnage, Argyll landed his second son, Charles, to rally the clansmen, after which he proceeded to Campbeltown, where

TARBERT ON CORONATION DAY, 9ᵀᴴ AUGUST, 1902.

he published a strongly-worded declaration against the Government, and summoned to arms all the Campbells from sixteen to sixty; the isthmus of Tarbert, "a very centrical place," being fixed upon as the rendezvous. The Earl soon learned, however, that the action of the Government had already taken the spirit out of his clansmen; and, although the fiery cross was hurried over hill and dale throughout his territories, the response was sadly inadequate to the work on hand.

Other circumstances threatened to render abortive the effort ere it had well begun. These had their foundation in the fact that Argyll's supreme position was only nominal, and all questions regarding the expedition were determined by a meddlesome committee of five, who set themselves diligently to devise means of limiting his power and controlling his movements. At Campbeltown, encouraging reports having been received from the Lowlands, Sir John Cochrane, Sir Patrick Hume, and others, "ernestly pressed the Erle that wee might divide, and some of us go thither; he seemed satisfied, but withal, told us that his son, Charles, and other gentlemen, were at Tarbot Castle with 1200 men, and if we would saile the ships thither, and many boats wee had, he with Sir John [Cochrane] and a good pairt of the sogers would take a land march through Kantire, levie the whole country, and joine them, and that we might then goe to the Lowlands with a considerable division of men . . . So he marched, and we sailed; came to Tarbot, and found our friends at a rendezvous here. We made of horse and foot 1800 men."

The disappointment experienced by the Earl as he contemplated the limited response to his summons must have been keen indeed. In earlier and more prosperous times a Mac Calein Mor could easily have raised 5000 or 6000 claymores, but so many chieftains and heads of houses had been thrown into prison, and so seriously had their territories been ravaged, that the spirit of the Clan Campbell was broken.

Tarbert was reached by Argyll on the 27th May, and here he printed a declaration rebutting the assertions of his enemies as to self-seeking, protesting that his intention was to secure the freedom of his country from the tyrannical rule of a Papist king, and inviting and entreating all honest Protestants, and particularly all his friends and blood relations, to concur with him and his coadjutors in his present undertaking.

But it was not alone the opposition and insinuations of his enemies that the Earl had to face, but the bickerings and opposition of his Lowland allies, which became aggravated at Tarbert to a degree he had never experienced before. As the result of these differences the immediate procedure took the form of

a compromise, and it was arranged that Argyll should begin operations in the Highlands, while Hume and Cochrane with a part of
the forces should proceed to the Lowlands and endeavour to rally
the Hill-men to their banner. The latter was a futile effort, for the
coast of Ayrshire was guarded by English frigates, and the expedition
returned to Argyll without having secured any accession of force.

The ultimate fate of this ill-starred expedition is too well known
to require lengthened mention here. On the 29th May, two days
after his arrival at the castle, the Earl "loosed from the Tarbet and
came into the town of Rosa in the isle of Boot, where he took a
night's provision for himself and his men." Some of the party had
a successful skirmish at Greenock, when they "tooke some meal out
of a girnull and a pretty barque out of the harbour, and returned to
Rothesay, While wee were away" continues the writer, "the Erle
had caused burn the Castle, because a house of his had been burnt
in Cowall."

RECREATION GROUNDS ON CORONATION DAY.

Opposed in his plan of campaign by his Lowland allies, faced by
shortness of provisions on account of their mismanagement of the
commissariat, and threatened by overwhelming forces on sea and land,
Argyll evaded the king's ships and landed in Dumbartonshire. At Kil-
patrick, his little army was broken up on the 18th June; and at Inch-
innan, on the Cart, he was seized by a party of militia and conveyed to

Edinburgh. On the 30th day of the same month, he was beheaded, dying like a Christian hero.

Deprivation of territory and offices and jurisdictions followed upon the execution of this chief of the Campbell clan. It was a serious blow to the house of Argyll, yet many a subordinate clan rejoiced with unbounded joy in their new-found freedom. But the whirligig of time brought, ere long, ample compensation to the great western clan; and, with the accomplishment of the Revolution in 1680, both place and power were again theirs.

"CORINTHIANS" CROSSING THE LINE.

The Tryst of Claverhouse at Tarbert.

For many months after the landing of William and Mary, the state of the country was extremely unsettled, and, as the chief support of James came from his co-religionists in Ireland, the district of Kintyre, from its nearness to Ireland, was looked upon as a convenient centre for the reception and transference of troops coming from that country. In May, 1689, the Committee of Estates, having received notice that "some Irishes" had landed in Kintyre, ordered the immediate concentration of a considerable body of troops at Tarbert. A month later (27th June) we find Viscount Dundee, commander of the forces that still adhered to James in Scotland, writing to Lord Melfort and appealing to him to send over some reinforcements from Ireland.

An Incident of the 'Forty Five'

After requesting that from 5000 to 6000 troops, including 600 or 800 horse, might be landed at Inverlochy, his letter proceeds:—"So soon as the boats return, let them ferry over as many more foot as they think fit to the Point of Kintyre, which will soon be done. . . I should march towards Kintyre, and meet at the neck of Tarbitt the foot, and so march to raise the country, and then towards the Passes of the Forth to meet the king." Whether or not Irish troops were sent to Kintyre cannot be gathered, but the "bloody Clavers" did not keep his tryst at Tarbert, for the fatal battle of Killiecrankie supervened, and he passed from the scene of mortal strife.

The Laird of Largie and the 'Forty-five.'

With the succeeding efforts in 1715 and 1745 in favour of Jacobitism, the history of Tarbert is but lightly associated, the lairds of the village and its neighbourhood having espoused the Hanoverian cause. One incident, however, regarding the '45 may here be referred to. Cuthbert Bede, in his "Glencreggan," gives the following version on the authority of the late Laird of Largie:—"In the 'Forty-live,' the then Laird of Largie was for going out. He was to join with other lairds in taking ship at Tarbert. The minister of Kilcalmonell [Clachan] invited him to spend the night at the manse on his way to Tarbert, and by the over-exercise of hospitality contrived that Largie should be late in getting up next morning. And so it happened that when Largie arrived at Tarbert with his contingent the fleet had sailed. Thus was the property of Largie saved in '45. Afterwards Largie went to Paris and gave great entertainments to the Prince, whereby he got so much into debt as to be obliged to sell a portion of his estates." From another source he received this second version of the story:—"In the 'Forty-five,' the proprietors of Kintyre raised their men against Prince Charlie, but Macdonald of Largie declared for the Prince. Upon this, the Laird of Tarbert sent him word that if he intended to join the Prince he would meet him on his way in passing, and that they would have a hot day of it, and that few Macdonalds should remain to join any party. On this the Laird of Largie thought fit to change his mind, so he sent his men with the rest of the men of Kintyre" to Inverary.

The Old Lairds of Tarbert—The McAlisters.

The McAlisters—the Clan Ian Dubh—appear to have been descended from Alexander, a younger son of Donald (progenitor of the McDonalds) son of Reginald, who was second son of the "mighty Somerled," Regulus of Argyll. The old genealogies, however, indicate also another possible line of descent, viz., from Alexander, son of Angus Mor and grandson of Donald.

In the "Register of the Privy Seal" for the year 1515 appears the name of "Angus Vic Ean Dubh." This Angus, who was chief of the McAlisters, and Laird of Loup (an estate in Kintyre, ten miles from Tarbert), had three sons, the second of whom, Donald, founded the Tarbert branch of the clan, and was constable of the castle.

Next to the McAlisters of Loup, the McAlisters of Tarbert would seem to have been the most important branch of the clan, and they were during several centuries the hereditary constables of the castle of Tarbert. According to the "Statistical Account of Scotland," published in 1794, the McAlisters of Tarbert had been, in the hey-day of their power, "by far the most considerable family in South Knapdale." They also held much land in Kintyre. Although descended from the McDonalds, all their lands were held on feu charters granted by the Argylls. In their more prosperous days almost all the lands for some miles around Tarbert were in their possession, while northward their territory extended along the coasts of Loch Fyne and Loch Gilp to the extremity of South Knapdale parish.

From references existing in several authorities to the successors of Donald, we find the following mentioned as subsequent lairds. Charles was in possession in 1580, and Archibald, who was concerned in some raids into Bute in 1602, was at that time the heir apparent. In the years 1667 and 1678, Ronald was laird, and at these dates he was Commissioner of Supply for the shire of Argyll. The next to whom reference is made is a second Archibald. He was in possession in 1685, and in his favour an Act for the institution of fairs in the village was passed by the Scottish Parliament in the year 1705. Charles, the successor of the above, died in the year 1741, and was buried in the churchyard of Tarbert. On a marble tablet set in the wall surrounding the tomb may be read the following inscription to his memory and to that of his wife, who was a daughter of Walter Campbell of Skipness:—

S. M.
CAROLI McALISTER
de Tarbert
Qui obiit 3 us. Ap. 1741
Ætat.
ANNA CAMPBELL
Filia Gualteri Campbell
de Skipnefs,
tum ejus Conjux
hoc Monumentum
pofuit

Archibald, who succeeded to the estates, was the last of his line to inherit them.

DRILL HALL AND LIBRARY.

In military affairs of imperial interest, the McAlisters would appear to have been usually on the side favoured by their superiors, the Argylls. Like other clans, however, in those days when might was right, they had their own feuds and skirmishes with their neighbours. From their geographical position, the Tarbert branch of the clan were well placed either for holding their own or for making forays by sea or land upon adjacent territories.

On one occasion they were called upon to repel an invasion of the McIvers, which resulted in a "bloody conflict." A branch of the McIvers having settled at Lochgilp, and built a small fort on the west side of it, made many raids on their southern neighbours. As the result of two encounters, however, they were eventually almost exterminated. The first of these occurred with the M'Neils near the mouth of West Loch Tarbert; the second was the occasion referred to above, in which they were seriously defeated by the McAlisters of Tarbert, on the shores of Loch Fyne.

Arran was a favourite scene for the forays of the Knapdale and Kintyre men; and, from the "Register of the Privy Council," we gather that complaints against the authors of these forays were frequently made to the Government by the proprietors of that picturesque island. In the raid into Bute in 1602, formerly referred to, Archibald McAlister, younger of Tarbert, was accompanied by Campbell of Auchinbreck; Colin Campbell, younger of Kilberry; McNeil of Taynish, and other gentlemen, with a following of about 1200 men.

During the confiscation of Argyll towards the close of the seventeenth century, when the followers of Athole were plundering the Campbells in wholesale fashion, Archibald McAlister, the then laird of Tarbert, also seized the opportunity that presented itself of making frequent raids on the territory of his former feudal superior. Issuing from the shelter of the castle, Innellan and Colintraive on the one hand and Inverary on the other, were laid under contribution; and the paper, entitled, "Depredations committed on the Clan Campbell in 1685 and 1686," is very illuminating as bringing home to us not only the lack of respect for the property of others which characterised the good people of those days, but also the miscellaneous nature of the goods which were "lifted" in such wholesale fashion. Horses, cows, sheep, geese, money, a ferry-boat (Colintraive), a gray plaid, a dirk, plough irons, hides, an anchor tow, herring nets, meal, an axe, brewing graith, barrels (empty and full), tables, chests, doors, a pot and crook, a brass pan, a standing bed, and other household plenishings were among the goods with which the inhabitants of Tarbert enriched themselves, at the expense of their neighbours.

The disastrous effects of such raids on the country were frequently borne home to the Governments of those days, and, with a view to fostering the arts of peace, establishing friendly intercourse, and furthering civilisation, many means were had recourse to from time

NET-DRYING AT TARBERT.

to time. Among these was the establishment of fairs and markets in central localities. In September, 1705, an Act was passed by the Scottish Parliament in favour of Archibald M'Alister, instituting "four yearly fairs and a weekly mercat at the toun of East Tarbet." The weekly market was to be held on Tuesdays, and each of the four fairs was to last two days. These latter were to begin respectively on 10th May, 16th July, 19th August, and 16th October. None of these dates, it will be observed, corresponds with that on which the yearly fair has been so long held, viz., the last Thursday in July—an occasion which is made much of by the inhabitants of Tarbert and a wide district around. The above Act was among the last passed by the Parliament of Scotland.

Not many years after the institution of these fairs and markets evil days overlook the McAlisters of Tarbert. From some cause or other Archibald McAlister had become financially straitened. His lands were heavily mortgaged, and by degrees passed into other hands, so that some years before the middle of the eighteenth century, the ancient stock ceased to be the possessors of a single acre. Dael and Craiglass became the property of Mr Macarthur Stewart, of Milton, and the other lands north of Inverneil fell to Mr Peter Dow Campbell, of Kildusclan (a title taken from the name of a small chapel on the shore of Lochgilp). Four farms constituting the Erines estate became possessed by Mr McFarlane of Muckroy; three more were formed into the estate of Kintarbert, and became the property of Campbell of Kintarbert; while the remainder of the original estate, with the mansion house which was situated at Barmore, just below the position occupied by the present residence, was purchased in 1746 by Archibald Campbell of Stonefield.

Argyll's Lawsuit with McAlister's Creditors.

By this time Tarbert Castle had fallen seriously into disrepair, and this fact, together with others that shall appear, formed the subject of an important and unique lawsuit which Argyll instituted in the year 1762 against the creditors of the last McAlister laird, and which may be here referred to.

While the McAlisters were yet in prosperous circumstances, they had built for themselves the mansion house at Barmore, spoken of above; and the castle being no longer required to serve its original purpose of a fort, its condition was neglected, contrary to the stipulations of the old charter. The original of the charter is in Latin. The following excerpt contains the points on which the action was based. It is of interest as showing to some extent the conditions on which the Tarbert estate was held.

It stipulates that the vassal should provide:—

"A boat of six oars in time of peace and war, which they shall be bound to equip properly with arms and all necessaries, along with six rowers and a steersman for the service of our S. D. N. . . . lord the king, and us and our heirs and descendants for transporting us and our aforesaids from Tarbert to Strondour, Silver-craigs, and Lochgear; and likewise to any part of Cowal between the promontory of Aird and the Strait of Ottar, at the cost and expense of the said Archd. McAlister and his heirs, as often as required. And likewise the said Archibald McAlister and his aforesaids shall be bound faithfully, steadfastly, and securely to watch, ward, and defend the said castle and fortalice for the use and service of us and our aforesaids from the attacks of our enemies and foes, and to receive and guard prisoners in the said castle at the expense of us and our afore-saids, whenever they receive a command from us or our aforesaids, or our deputies from time to time. And that they will be faithful and obedient unto us and our aforesaids in all other things incumbent on the office of keeper of the said castle, as the other captains and keep-ers of our other castles and houses within the shire of Argyll shall be

CARNBAN.

bound and are wont to do. And likewise to preserve and maintain the said castle of Tarbert wind and water tight in all time coming at the cost and expense of the said Archibald McAlister and his aforesaids, and to receive and entertain us and our aforesaids, whenever we come to the said castle, in the same manner as the other keepers of our castles are wont to do."

In prosecuting his suit before the Lords of Ses-sion, Argyll admitted that certain of the obligations could not then be lawfully enforced, and on these clauses he did not ask for judgment in his favour.

The Lords found as follows:—

"That the pursuer's vassal in the Estate of Tarbert is bound upon his own proper charges and expenses to keep and uphold a boat of six oars, and to provide the same with six rowers and a steersman and all things necessary for the use of the superior and his family, in terms of the former feu charters thereof; and also to keep the mansion house now built upon said estate wind and water light; and find that the prestations are not personal services, and do not fall under the statute of George I. founded on, [by the defenders], but that the future feu rights of said estate ought to be burdened therewith, and to contain a reddendo in these terms; and remit to the Lord Ordinary to proceed accordingly. But with respect to that part of the reddendo of the former charters whereby the vassal is bound to receive and entertain the superior and his heirs, gratis, in his Castle of Tarbert in the same way as the other Keepers of the Pursuer's Castles are bound to do, they remit to the Lord Ordinary to hear parties further, and do therein as he shall see cause."

This decision was, at the time, considered of much importance, and it became a precedent governing future actions of a similar nature.

Though landless, many descendants of the old family continue to live in the village and neighbourhood. Others have gone from the home of their fathers, and several fill honourable positions in the professions and in other spheres. The brilliant career of Dr Donald McAlister, appointed early in 1907 to the Principalship of Glasgow University, has been a source of the liveliest interest and satisfaction to the good people of the village. His father, Mr Donald McAlister, a representative of the ancient family, was born in Tarbert, though the future principal first saw the light in Perth.

Herschel Prizeman at Cambridge in 1876, and Senior Wrangler and First Smith Prizeman the following year, Dr McAlister has since proved himself one of the most versatile of men— scientist, mathematician, and linguist—and to be possessed of intellectual gifts of the very highest order. Broad-minded and of great force of character, he has filled with splendid distinction many high positions, and won many honours. In addition to his principalship, he holds the distinguished position of President of the General Medical Council, and in his new sphere much is expected of him as a man of the widest knowledge in matters educational, and as an organiser and administrator of proved ability.

John Y. W. McAlister, younger brother of the Principal, holds the office of Secretary and Consulting Librarian to the Royal Society of Medicine, London, and is editor of *The Library*, a very successful quarterly publication.

THE HARBOUR FROM THE NORTH.

The Campbells of Stonefield, Lairds of Tarbert.

Archibald Campbell, of Stonefield, who purchased in 1746 the larger part of McAlister's estate, and whose descendants continue still in possession, was a cadet of the house of Lochnell. By the male line the family is descended from John Gorm, second son of Colin, third Earl of Argyll, while by the female side they trace their descent from the Breadalbane stock through Sir John Campbell of Glenorchy, father of the first Earl of Breadalbane. The title of "Stonefield" is derived from the name of an estate which they formerly possessed on the picturesque shores of

Loch Etive. It is now known by its Gaelic name of Auchnacloich, meaning Stonefield.

After selling their estates in that region, as well as some possessions in the island of Lismore, the Stonefields became connected with the Tarbert district as early as the year 1716 or 1717, by the purchase from the Campbells of Blythswood of a portion of their present estate situated to the south and west of Bardaravine Burn. At this period the family were also possessed of estates in the Parish of Kilmaronock, in the north of Dumbartonshire, while about the same time as they purchased the above land in the vicinity of Tarbert they became proprietors of the estate of Strathleven (then called Stonefield), situated in the neigbourhood of the town of Dumbarton.

Archibald Campbell was a man of much ability. During the affair of the "Forty-Five" he was Sheriff of Argyle, and by him it was that information was first sent to the Government of the arrival and landing of the Prince.

After the abolition of hereditary jurisdictions in 1748 he was appointed Deputy-Sheriff of Argyle and Bute, at the yearly salary of £250 sterling. This position he retained for many years. In the conduct of his private affairs he showed much energy, and did much to improve his estate. By enclosing, and draining, and planting extensively he increased its value very considerably, and did splendid work in connection with the making and improvement of the roads round about Tarbert. His energy and determination are well illustrated by an incident relating to the making of the road between Ardrishaig and Tarbert, which is given in the "New Statistical Account":—

"The Sliabh Gaoil road, which was so useful before the introduction of steam, and conferred such a boon on the country generally, and on Kintyre particularly, was obtained through the instrumentality of Sheriff Campbell, one of the ancestors of the present family of Stonefield. The line was surveyed by an English engineer. It is said that he attempted to travel over the ground; but the rocks were so precipitous, the ferns so gigantic, the Englishman so unwieldy and so unaccustomed to travel such rough grounds, that, after much tumbling and scrambling, he was obliged to betake himself to his boat, and finish his survey by rowing along the shore. On arriving at Barmore House, the residence of Sheriff Campbell, he remarked to the Sheriff that if was a hopeless thing to attempt opening a road along the projected line; that it was an undertaking fit for the Empress Catherine of Russia, and not fit for private individuals. The Sheriff ordered his clerk or treasurer to pay the English surveyor for his trouble, and with that determination and resolution which so much characterised that gentleman, the Sheriff set about the mighty task of opening the Sliabh Gaoil road, and persevered till it was finished. . . . .

Before the opening of this road, the district of Kintyre was quite insulated from the rest of Argyllshire. The only path by which any communication between the two places could be maintained was almost quite impassable. It ran along hills and dales which were intersected by water courses without any bridges. In summer the waters were fordable, but in winter the attempt to cross them was both difficult and dangerous. "

OPENING OF RECREATION GROUNDS PAVILION, 26ᵀᴴ APRIL, 1901.

In carrying out this costly but useful undertaking, Stonefield was ably assisted by His Grace the Duke of Argyll, and many gentlemen of the shire, who contributed liberally towards its accomplishment.

Archibald Campbell died in the year 1777, and was buried at Airidh-Mhor (then called Stonefield), where was an early residence of the family. He was succeeded in the estates by his son John, judiciallystyled

Lord Stonefield. A daughter, Elizabeth, married John Campbell of Carwhin, and became the mother of the fourth earl and first marquis of Breadalbane.

Lord Stonefield was an eminent judge: "Admitted advocate in 1748, he was elevated to the bench of the Court of Session in 1762. In 1787 he succeeded Lord Gardenstone as a lord of justiciary, which appointment, however, he resigned in 1792, retaining his seat in the Court of Session till his death, 19th June, 1801, having been thirty-nine years a judge of the Supreme Court. By his wife, Lady Grace Stuart, daughter of James, second Earl of Bute, and sister of the Prime Minister, John, third earl, Lord Stonefield had seven sons, all of whom predeceased him." Colin, his eldest son, was Colonel of the Dumbarton Fencibles, which regiment he was instrumental in raising in the year 1794.

Lord Stonefield's second son, John, was the hero of Mangalore, the soldier whose memorable defence of that town from May, 1783, to January of the following year, first arrested the victorious career of Tippoo Sultan, son of Hyder Ali. Major Campbell, who had already distinguished himself in several engagements, was in 1783 appointed to the provisional command of the British forces in the Bidnure country, and soon found himself called upon to defend the important fortress of Mangalore against the prodigious army of Tippoo Sultan. The latter's forces were estimated at 140,000 men, with a hundred pieces of artillery, and the defence of the town by Major Campbell with a garrison numbering only 1883, of whom but two or three hundred were British soldiers, "is justly reckoned one of the most remarkable achievements that ever distinguished the British arms in India."

During the siege, breach after breach was made, which the besiegers attempted to storm, but they were invariably driven back at the point of the bayonet. Twice did Colonel McLeod appear off the port, with ships filled with troops, but instead of proceeding to attack Tippoo in his camp, he made agreements with that barbarian for permission for the garrison to procure supplies, which agreements Tippoo implemented in his own fashion by ordering all persons to sell the besieged nothing but damaged and putrid stores.

The Hero of Mangalore

The bravery and resolution displayed by Major Campbell were so much admired by Tippoo that he expressed a wish to see him. The Major, accompanied by several of his officers, accordingly waited upon Tippoo, when "he presented to each of them a handsome shawl; and after their return to the fort, he sent Major Campbell an additional present of a very fine horse, which the famishing garrison afterwards killed and ate."

After great suffering from their eight months' siege, the garrison capitulated on the 24th January, 1784, on the understanding that they should march out with all the honours of war. Accordingly the fort was evacuated on the 30th, the garrison, reduced to 856, embarking for Tillicherry, on the coast of Malabar. A few

STONEFIELD HOUSE.

weeks later, Lieutenant-Colonel Campbell, shattered in health by the fatigues and privations sustained during the siege, quitted the army and retired to Bombay, where he died on the 23rd March, in the 31st year of his age. Lord Stonefield was offered a baronetcy in recognition of his son's brilliant services. By order of the East India Company, a monument was erected to Colonel Campbell's memory in the church of Bombay, testifying to the merits of the distinguished young soldier, and recording their appreciation of his important services to his country. The author's brother, Dr. Trafford Mitchell, when on a visit to India in 1886 visited the church, and viewed with interest the memorial which commemorates the bravery and worth of one whose memory the people of Tarbert do well to cherish.

Lord Stonefield, having been predeceased by all his sons, was succeeded in the possession of the estates by his grandson, John, eldest son of Colonel Colin Campbell, already referred to. A few years before the accession of John (1792), the old mansion-house, built by the McAlisters at Barmore, was burnt down by accident. The present handsome residence, which occupies a site on a somewhat higher level than the former house, was built by laird John in 1837. The doorway is surmounted by the Campbell coat of arms, and on either side is quaintly inscribed the text: "Thou shalt love the Lord thy God with all thy heart, and thy neighbour as thy self." Paintings by Nasmyth, of the adjoining scenery, adorn the walls of the ante-room, and examples of Sir Joshua Reynolds and Vandyck, and numerous family portraits, reaching back to the days of armour, are among the art treasures which the dining-room and drawing-room contain.

Ere he died on March 18th, 1857, John Campbell effected many important improvements on the estate. He was buried in the new family mausoleum, situated half-a-mile to the north of the house. By his wife, Wilhelmina, daughter of Sir James Colquhoun, Bart. of Colquhoun and Luss, he left two sons, Colin George Campbell, born in 1811, and James Colquhoun Campbell, D.D., born in 1813. The latter, having graduated in honours at Trinity College, Cambridge, was successively appointed rector of Merthyr Tydvil and Archdeacon of Llandaff; and in April, 1859, became Lord Bishop of Bangor on the nomination of Lord Derby. He died in November, 1895, and was buried on the 13th of that month in the family vaults at Stonefield.

Colin George Campbell, who became laird on the death of his father in 1857, was for many years Convener of the County of Argyll and a Deputy Lieutenant. To his enlightened policy Tarbert owes many improvements, and notably the erection of the pier and the formation of the pier road. By him also Garbhal was planted in 1867-8. By his wife, Elizabeth, daughter of Gibbon Fitzgibbon, of Ballyseeda, Ireland, he had three sons, John, Colin George, and Henry Osborne, and two daughters, Elizabeth Ida, and Jane Arabella. He died on 25th July, 1887, and was buried at Stonefield, deeply lamented by the community.

John Campbell, who should have succeeded to the estates, predeceased his father, having died on 24th January, 1885, at the early age of 39. His wife was Adela Harriet Pelham Clinton, daughter of Lord Charles Clinton. By her he had two sons, Colin George Pelham and Nigel Leslie, and one daughter, Sybil Adela.

Colin George Pelham Campbell, J.P. and D.L., the present laird, was married on the 15th November, 1893, to the Lady Ileene Frances Cairns Hastings, second daughter of the 13th Earl of Huntingdon. For many years the laird has taken a keen interest in local affairs, and in the volunteers in particular; and since the death of Mr J. Windsor Stuart he has been in command of the Argyll and Bute Royal Garrison Artillery Volunteers.

FROM THE CASTLE HILL.

"Dream no more of southern rambles!
Snowy Alp or Castled Rhine;
Step on board the good Columba,
Book for Tarbert on Loch Fyne ! "

In the year 1836 Lord Teignmouth published a work in two volumes entitled "Sketches of the Coasts and Islands of Scotland." These sketches were the outcome of tours made by him in those disticts in the years 1827 and 1829. On both occasions his Lordship spent some time in Tarbert, and from his pages we glean several items regarding the village which are of considerable interest.

Of his visit in 1827 Lord Teignmouth writes thus: "Crossing the entrance of Loch Fine we entered the romantic little harbour of East Loch Tarbert, the headquarters of the celebrated herring-fishery. The rude out-work of its rocks apparently barring access; the overhanging keep of its ruined castle; the village, and the innumerable fishing boats choking up every nook and crevice, formed a scene singularly picturesque, the effect of which is heightened by the method in which the fishermen hang their nets." He describes the nets as being hung not only on poles along the shore, but also on cross poles on the boats, as is still sometimes done on drift-net boats.

Fifty years earlier Pennant was also impressed by the "rude out-work of its rocks" which guards the sheltered bay. In his "Tour" he writes: "On the northern side of the entrance of the harbour the rocks are of a most grotesque form; vast fragments piled on each other, the faces contorted and undulated in such figures as if created by fusion of matter after some intense heat, yet did not appear to me a lava, or any suspicion of having been the recrement of a volcano." If the curious in such matters will visit Garbhal Point (*Garbhalach*, "rocky") they will readily understand the distinguished traveller's reference. The unique character of the village and its surroundings likewise impressed McCulloch on his western Tour: "The village and bay of Tarbert," he writes, "form a very singular spot, wild alike and unexpected." Even at the present day no one can look upon Tarbert for the first time without experiencing the same feelings: quaintness, picturesqueness, and wildness of aspect being still its most characteristic features.

The Old Homesteads.

Down to the close of the eighteenth century the village proper consisted, essentially, of what is now the Back Street; but numerous groups of cottages on the outskirts had the little town as a common centre, and thus its importance was added to. Some of these old homesteads still exist and flourish, while others are only a memory. It is interesting to recall the old Gaelic names, and to search out their meaning. Such groups existed at *Maoldarach*, "the oaken or hard headland"; *Breaclurach*, "the spotted ruin," situated above the pier; *Baluachdruch*, "the high township"; *Bruachnasugh*, "the berry brae"; *Goirtean-na-chuileann*, "the little holly field"; *Achadh-nu-glaic*, "the field of the narrow glen;" *Lagluinge*, "the ship-hollow"; *Carnban*, "the white cairn"; *Glenakill*, "the glen of the church or burying ground"; West Tarbert; *Eascairt*, "the stream by the stone" (the reference probably being to the Standing Stones, of which there are still five close by the house); *Dubhcladach*, "the black shore"; *Abbainn-nan-gillean*, "the young men's river"; *Glenralloch*, "the glen between two lochs"; *Burran*, "the high place with the water"; *Barfad*, "the long summit or ridge"; *Barmore*, " the great summit or ridge."

COTTAGE AT BALUACHDRACH.

Modern Developments,

With the beginning of the nineteenth century Tarbert began to develop along modern lines, and houses sprang up in increasing number around the margin of the inner bay. About the same time (1809) a memorial was presented to the Parliamentary Commissioners, in which it was stated that the village of Tarbert was "one of the most considerable places in the West Highlands, on account of the excellence of its harbour and the peculiar advantages of its locality. It is the centre of communication between the numerous sea-lochs that indent the coast of this part of the country, and offers great facilities of transit between the districts on the east and west." The purpose of this memorial was to induce the Government of the day to undertake the renewal of the land breast-work originally constructed by the proprietor, and the enlargement of the quay.

In reply the Commissioners "agreed to the enlargement of the quay, the renewing of the landbreast, which had become ruinous, and the improvement of the approaches to the harbour by the removal of some rocks obstructing the entrance." After the lapse of a century these structures continue in good repair, and have proved a boon of no ordinary character to the villagers. A quarter of a century ago a considerable widening of the roadway between the Old Quay and the "New Quay" (that referred to in the memorial) was effected by the then laird, and two years since the "New Quay" was considerably extended and much improved, but otherwise the work accomplished by the Commissioners has remained to this day as it left the workmen's hands.

Early Steamers on Loch Fyne.

It is probable that the improvements in the harbour above referred to were not yet completed when the first steamer entered the bay of Tarbert. Up to this period communication with the ports on the Firth of Clyde were regularly kept up by a sailing packet, but remarkable developments were at hand. In August, 1812, the *Comet*, the first steamer to ply on European waters, began to run between Glasgow and Greenock. A few weeks later, "on the 2nd September, the sailings of the *Comet* were extended *via* Tarbert and the Crinan Canal, to Oban, Port Appin, and Fort William, the return journey occupying four days."

A few years later the first *Inveraray Castle*, built in 1814, was engaged in the Loch Fyne trade, while the second *Comet*, built in 1821, was, like the first of the name, on the West Highland route. *Inveraray Castle* No. 2 was built in 1820, and the *Toward Castle* in 1822. In 1829, the date of Lord Teignmouth's second visit, daily communication between Glasgow and Inveraray, calling at Tarbert, was kept up by the *Dunoon Castle* and the *Rothesay Castle*. Occasionally the *Inveraray Castle* No. 2 and the *Toward Castle* were employed on the same route. Other early boats were the *James Ewing*, the *St. Catherine*, and the *Tarbert Castle*. The latter, built in 1836, was, after a short term of service, wrecked on Ardmarnock beach. Her engines, however, were afterwards fitted on board *Inveraray Castle* No. 3, which was built in 1839, and continued on the route for over fifty years. Among later boats were the *Windsor Castle*, built in 1845 (afterwards re-named the *Mary Jane* and the *Glencoe*) and the *Duntroon Castle*. In connection with the latter steamer it is told that on one occasion when the bellman of Inveraray was going through the town intimating her departure he informed the good people that "God-willing and weather permitting the *Duntroon Castle* would leave Inveraray Pier on Monday morning at six o'clock, and on Tuesday whether or no!"

FORMER PARISH CHURCH. BUILT 1775.

In the year 1844, the *Cardiff Castle* was built to the order of the Castle Steam Packet Co., and by this steamer the famous Royal Route was inaugurated. Among the owners were the well-known William

Campbell of Tullichewan and James Hunter of Hafton. In connection with this route the name *Iona* first appears in 1855, when *Iona*, No. 1 was built to the order of David Hutcheson & Co. *Iona*, No. 2 was launched in 1863. Like its predecessor it had a short career, and was succeeded in 1864 by *Iona*, No. 3, the favourite steamer of the present day. In 1878 the majestic *Columba* was placed upon the route.

East Loch Tarbert, which constitutes the harbour, is an arm of Loch Fyne, seven furlongs in length and three furlongs in breadth at its widest part, with an island about its centre dividing the harbour into an inner and an outer portion. Than the inner portion, approached by tortuous channels on both sides of the island, no harbour could be more secure. Unfortunately, on account of the very considerable silting up and filling in that has occurred since the work of the Commissioners was completed, the approach to the breast work has become so shallow that the innermost parts of the harbour are much less fitted for their purpose than formerly.

Within recent years the desirability of deepening the harbour to such an extent as shall ensure that the shore will be covered at all states of the tide has been often under the consideration of the inhabitants, and, with the coming of better times, it will doubtless be effected at no distant date. When it is accomplished, not only will the harbour be more useful, but the attractiveness of Tarbert as a watering place and summer resort will be enormously enhanced, and the well-being of the inhabitants correspondingly prompted.

It is interesting to find at what an early date (1827) Tarbert was able to attract summer visitors to its shores, and hills, and sheltered seas. This fact, together with several other illuminating items, is brought out in the following quotation from Lord Teignmouth:—"This little port," he writes, "contains a respectable inn, and a few comfortable lodginghouses for the use of the *salt-water* people, as persons who visit the coast for sea bathing are usually called in these parts. A long row of low huts on the shore attracted our notice; the interior of one was remarkably neat and clean, belying the squalidness of its exterior. It proved to be one of the Society's schools;

or schools maintained by the joint contributions of the Society for Promoting Christian Knowledge, established at Edinburgh, which pays the salary of the schoolmaster amounting to £25; and of the heritor or landed proprietor on whose estate the school is found, who furnishes the house and garden; and of the scholars themselves, who pay certain fees. In this little seminary two boys formed a Latin class, . . . and two were studying Greek." The latter two were sons of a farmer and an exciseman respectively, and were going forward to the Church.

This school-house on the shore, the site of which we cannot identify, was after a time replaced by a building erected by the General Assembly of the Church of Scotland, which still stands in front of the Established Church. It is now used as a dwellinghouse.

PARISH CHURCH. BUILT 1886.

The older inhabitants will also recall the school conducted so long by Ronald McAlister at Lochend, near the entrance to Glenralloch. Here many of the young men of Tarbert, who afterwards followed the sea, received such a knowledge of navigation as fitted them to fill important positions in the mercantile marine of our country. These schools were supplemented after the Disruption by the Free Church School which met in the vestibule of the church up to the year 1864. In that year the central portion of the school buildings now in use was erected by the congregation at a cost of £600, and the school was transferred thence. When in 1872 School Boards came into being, this building was generously handed over to the community for the sum of £94, which sum was paid to the congregation in name of furniture. Since that time, many additions have been made to the structure, which is now large and up to date.

Matters Ecclesiastical.

Situated as Tarbert is, partly in the district of Kintyre and partly in that of Knapdale—districts separated by a tiny stream—its ecclesiastical affairs were for long under the control of the ministers and sessions of the United Parishes of Kilcalmonell and Kilberry, and the Parish of Knapdale—later of South Knapdale. it is surmised that at an early date there was a chapel at Glenakill; and, as we have seen, there was in Bruce's day, and during the reign of James IV., a chapel in connection with the castle, but for centuries the village and neighbourhood were dependent on the occasional ministrations of the Parish ministers, who resided, one at Clachan, and the other (latterly) at Achahoish, 20 miles distant.

Where the services were conducted previous to the year 1775 we cannot tell, but in that year a church was erected on the site of the present church, " and a missionary established there by the Society for Propagating Christian Knowledge." In the year 1864 the church was endowed, and raised from the position of a mission station to that of a *Quoad Sacra* Parish, while in 1886 the old building was demolished, and was replaced by the present imposing and very handsome edifice, which is seated for 600.

With the Disruption in 1843 came the erection in Church Street of the old Free Church, now neglected and decayed. The new church, with its spire rising to the height of 110 feet, was built in 1896 on the site of the old thatched cottage which, it is understood, was in earlier times used as a court-house in connection with the Sheriffdom of Tarbert. The new building, Gothic in its leading characteristics, is a handsome structure, seated for 700, and is now the property of the "Legal Frees." The ministers of both churches enjoy commodious manses, that of the Established Church being situated on the isthmus and close by the church, while that of the Free Church looks down on the village from the north.

Census Returns of Fifty Years

The United Free section of the old congregation, which has been homeless since the announcement in August, 1904, of the House of Lords decision in the great Church case, has already secured a manse for their minister on the shores of Maoldarach Bay, and is pushing forward with the erection of it new church, which will provide 425 sittings.

OLD FREE CHURCH. BUILT 1843.

Recent Developments.

In his Report for the New Statistical Account, written about the year 1840, Rev. John McArthur, minister of Clachan, speaks of Tarbert as "a thriving little place." The population he estimated at 700 or 800. Since that date considerable strides have been made, and the village has enjoyed periods, time and again, of undoubted prosperity. The census returns of the Registration District over the last fifty years are as follows:—

1861 ... Pop. 1661	1891 ... Pop. 2208
1871 ... Pop. 1866	1901 ... Pop. 2128
1881 ... Pop. 2017	

During those years the population of the village has

increased to a larger extent than the above figures would appear to indicate, as there has been coincidently a considerable thinning out of the
people in the outlying parts of the district.

If we except the success of the herring fishing, which must always be the essential foundation of whatever measure of prosperity
Tarbert may possess, no circumstance has conduced so much to
the more modern development of the village as the construction
of the outer pier and the formation of the road leading to it. Up
to the year 1866, when these important improvements were made
by the Laird, Colin George Campbell, Esq. of Stonefield, at a cost
of £1600, passengers from Tarbert by sea had either to travel by

FREE CHURCH. BUILT 1896.

the cargo steamers — the good old *Mary Jane* or *Inverary Castle*, it
might be—which were slow, and frequently cumbered by cattle and
sheep, and by hundreds of herring boxes, or join the swift steamer

at the mouth of the harbour, by means of the well-remembered red ferry-boats, which started from the "New Quay." Neither method was at all satisfactory, and the inconvenience interfered seriously with the development of Tarbert.

That this was so was made evident by the rapid growth of the village which followed immediately on the erection of the outer pier, and the formation of the new road.

Previous to this date (1866) the road on the south side of the bay did not extend farther than the "New Quay;" and the two boat-building sheds of the village, and the greens on which nets were mended and set up, were approached by a narrow, rough path leading along the side of the castle-hill down on to Madabuidhe. The new road opened up feuing ground, which was speedily occupied, and Tarbert began to develop along new lines. A few years passed, and it was no longer simply a fishing village, quaint and picturesque withal, attracting a few summer visitors, and an occasional artist desirous of

THE NEW UNITED FREE CHURCH.

delineating on canvas its peculiar characteristics and charms. Year by year an increasing number of "salt-water people" sought accommodation, and year after year to meet this demand, as well as to gratify the taste for better houses which was coincidently being developed among the fishing population and others, cottages and villas sprang up in all directions, lining the new road, clothing the hill-sides, and leading to the formation of other new roads—Ileene Road on the north and Jubilee Road above the pier. It is interesting to reflect that a large proportion of these new houses are the property of fishermen.

The village is now one of the most progressive

and one of the most advanced in the Highlands. Its churches are handsome, and compare favourably with those of many towns of larger size; and its school—now higher grade—has for many years held a high place. Within the period referred to, the shops have been re-modelled, and are now unsurpassed among the smaller seaside resorts. The water supply from the Knapdale hills is ample and beyond reproach; the drainage is efficient, and is carried out into Loch Fyne; the roads are well kept, and seats have been provided for the use of visitors.

In other respects also the inhabitants have striven to make the town attractive alike to the resident and to the visitor. A Bowling Green and Tennis Courts have been in existence for several years, and a new 9-hole Golf Course has been laid out on the south side if the village, which it is expected will prove a great boon. A Library, which is largely used by visitors, is housed in the Drill Hall on the West Road, and the same building, as well as the Good Templars' Hall, built in 1872, is utilised for public meetings.

At no seaside resort is boating more safe than it is at Tarbert, and so sheltered is the harbour that it may be enjoyed at almost any time. Fishing with the handline on the banks, or with the fly along the rocky shore, or round the islands in the neighbourhood, often affords good sport, providing as a rule a toothsome breakfast for next morning.

The opportunities of bathing, however, are not what they ought to be. As a seaside resort Tarbert cannot afford to lag behind in this important matter. At a comparatively small cost the shores at several points might be easily cleared of boulders and rough stones, and good bathing ground provided. It would be a still further convenience were the stones utilised for the construction, here and there on the shore, of little piers for the use of small boats, as is already done at some parts.

Four Hotels, the "Tarbert," the "Columba," the "Commercial," and the "Victoria," provide for the comfort of the wayfarer, and worthily maintain the good name which the Hotels of Tarbert have so long enjoyed.

Branches of the Union and Clydesdale Banks afford the necessary facilities for the transaction of financial business.

Volunteering at Tarbert

The Drill Hall, referred to above, is the headquarters of the Tarbert Company (11th) of the Argyll and Bute Royal Garrison Artillery Volunteers. The Company took origin in the year 1866, when its captain was Colin George Campbell, Esq. of Stonefield, who had for lieutenants Messrs Hugh M'Lean and James E. McLarty. A few years later, John Campbell, younger of Stonefield, became captain in room of his father, and he continued in command until his untimely death on 24th January, 1885.

THE BATTERY AT MAOLDARACH.

Captain Campbell was succeeded in the command by Captain Alexander Mitchell, who, as a gunner, had joined the Company on its formation, and, since 1880, had acted as lieutenant to Captain Campbell. Captain Mitchell was awarded the V.D. in 1893, and retired in 1898 with the honorary rank of lieutenant-colonel. His successor in the command of the 11th Company was C. G. P. Campbell, Esq. of Stonefield, who retained the position until he was promoted to the command of the Corps in succession to the late Colonel J. Windsor Stuart. Since that date the headquarters of the Corps has been transferred from Rothesay to Tarbert.

The Tarbert Company, always zealous and patriotic, continues to maintain a vigorous existence under Captain Alexander McFarlane (who succeeded Colonel Campbell), with Mr J. S. Cavalier as lieutenant. In future they will form a Mountain Battery in the new Territorial Army.

Tarbert

" 'Tis on the waters that they toil,
And in the seas their harvests grow. "

While it is difficult to think of Tarbert without its castle and without those stirring associations which cluster around it, it is equally difficult to think of it apart from that great industry from which it still derives so much of its character. In days not so long gone by Tarbert was, not inaptly, known as the capital of herring-dom. Unfortunately, the title is at the present day by no means so appropriate, for within recent years hard times have overtaken the fishers of Loch Fyne.

How early in the history of our country Loch Fyne came into prominence as a fishing centre it is impossible to say, but the superior quality of its herring has been recognised and appreciated from a very early date. "More than a thousand years ago," says the author of "Glencreggan," "the fame of these Loch Fyne herring had spread far beyond Tarbert and the adjacent coasts, for in the year 836 the Netherlanders came to Loch Fyne to purchase the salted herrings. They were as cannie as the Scots, and they learnt the art and look up the trade of herring-curing. And they must have made the most of their knowledge as years went on, for in 1603 Sir Walter Raleigh speaks of the Dutch selling to other nations herrings that amounted in value to a million and a half of money, and, from first to last, employing two hundred thousand men in the herring trade, all these men being employed, and all these fish being caught on the coast of Scotland, and notably on Loch Fyne."

Some of our own early historians are also loud in their praise of Loch Fyne herring, and of Loch Fyne as a favourite haunt of the herring. "In Lochfine," says Hector Boece (1527) "is mair plente of hering than is in ony seis of Albion." Half a century later (1578) Bishop Leslie writes:—"In the Westir Seyes . . . the hail haruest and beginning of Winter is a gret schule of herring, bot in na place sa fatt and of sa pleisand a taste as in that loch mair Westirlie, quhilke afor we expremed vuder the name of [Loch] Fine." Proceeding, he refers to the great abundance of thin ill-conditioned herring on the Ayrshire coast at the end of winter and beginning of spring, thus making it apparent that then as now the Ballantrae banks were important spawning grounds.

Pennant on Drift-Net Fishing.

The date of their annual appearance in Loch Fyne has evidently been the same all down the centuries. Pennant, in his "Tour in Scotland" (1770) gives some interesting particulars of the characteristics of the Loch Fyne herring fishing in his day, and notes, as other writers do, the occasional absence of herring from these and other waters for prolonged periods:—"Lochfyne is noted for the vast shoals of herrings that appear here in July and continue till January. The highest is from September to Christmas, when near six hundred boats with four men in each are employed. A chain of nets is used (for several are united) of a hundred fathoms in length. As the herrings swim at very uncertain depths, so the nets are sunk to the depth the shoal

REDDING DRIFT NETS.

is found to take; the success therefore depends much on the judgment or good fortune of the fishers in taking their due depths, for it often happens that one boat will take multitudes while the next does not catch a single fish, which makes the boatmen perpetually enquire of each other about the depth of their nets. These are kept up by

buoys. . . . Sometimes the fish swim in twenty fathoms water, sometimes in forty, sometimes in fifty, and often times even at the bottom.
It is computed that each boat gets about £40 in the season. . . . The
present price is £1 4s. per barrel, but there is a drawback of the duty
on salt for those that are exported.

"The herring of Lochfyne are as uncertain in their migration as
they are on the coast of Wales. They had for numbers of years quitted that water, but appeared again there within these dozen years.
Such is the case with the lochs on all the western coast," etc., etc.

Here there is no mention of trawling, which probably up to that
time had not been practised, but our author's description of fishing
with the drift-net stands true of the method as worked at the present
day.

Prebendary William Gilpin, who visited upper Loch Fyne a few
years later than Pennant (1776) also gives us interesting material
for comparison between then and now:—"Lochfyne is one of the
favourite haunts of herring; and at certain seasons of the year is frequented by innumerable shoals. . . . At those seasons, they say, the
lake contains one part water, and two parts fish. In this single bay of
the lake, we were told that above six hundred boats are sometimes
employed in taking them. . . .

"The crews of these boats seem generally to be a cheerful, hap-
py race. Among the implements of each boat, the bagpipe is rarely
forgotten; the shrill melody of which you hear constantly resounding
from every part; except when all hands are at work. On Sunday, the
mirth of the several crews is changed into devotion: as you walk by
the side of the lake, if the evening be still, you hear them singing
psalms, instead of playing on the bagpipe."

Twenty years later, George Chalmers, in his "Caledonia"
(1807), tells the same cheering tale of plenty. "The value of the
herrings," he says, "which were caught in Loch Fyne in 1794 and
1795, has been computed at more than £40,000 each year," but
such great captures, he acknowledges, are very uncommon.

How often these bright and busy times came to the fishers of Loch Fyne
we have no means of knowing. They recall the halcyon days of forty to

forty-five years ago, when Tarbert harbour was literally packed with trawlers, drift-net boats, and curers; when riches rolled in upon the fishermen, and Tarbert enjoyed a measure of prosperity greater, probably, than it ever experienced before or since. As many as 700 boats might at that time be counted in the bay.

Lord Teignmouth, who visited Tarbert on several occasions in the years 1827 and 1829, gives, in his "Sketches" published in 1836, some welcome particulars regarding the fishing on Loch Fyne, and the habits of the fishermen at that date. Writing of the fishermen of Tarbert and the neighbouring coasts, he says:—"The outfit of a boat is expensive; the cost of it including rigging, varies from £30 to £50 and upwards, and may be estimated on the average at £40; and the price of a set of nets is £30, or £5 to a piece or barrel, of

PREPARING FOR SEA.

which six form a net. The usual length of the boat is twenty feet; it is built at Tarbert, Greenock, or Rothesay. It is furnished with three masts [there is evidently some mistake here as to the number of masts], a mainsail, a foresail, and a jib; and part of the bow is covered by a boarding or awning, in which bedding is placed. . . . Each boat is usually furnished with three men, one of whom is the master, who defrays the whole cost, and receives a double share of the profits of the fishing. He is also exempted by law from impressment. The proprietors of boats subscribe so much by the week to a fund, a species of insurance, out of which they are indemnified for the loss of their nets. The measure used is called a maize." From this description, it seems evident that the trawl net had not yet come into use in Loch Fyne.

Proceeding, he says:—"I was informed that any disputes arising among the fishermen were adjusted by arbitration, three seniors of the port performing this duty; an excellent practice." So also was the following:—"After supper, the fishermen not unfrequently kneel down to prayer, and sing a hymn, and when at home adopt the same rule."

We are prepared, however, to hear that in those days religion and whisky were closely associated. "There are," he writes, "no less than twenty public houses in Tarbert, which must be partly attributed to its being a great thoroughfare. The superintendent of the distillery at West Tarbert informed me that the fishermen carried out whisky to sea, observing emphatically, 'Sir, the Tarbert man must have his dram, let the world sink or swim.' "

The Rebel Trawlers of Tarbert.

For many years, the fishermen of Tarbert have been thorough-going trawlers. Forty-seven years ago, or thereby, this mode of fishing was declared illegal; but in spite of frequent imprisonments and numerous confiscations of boats and nets, most of the Tarbert men continued to prosecute trawling, and gunboats and special police (of whom for years there were eight in the village) endeavoured in vain to repress the system. The following dialogue, extracted from Black's "Princess of Thule," illustrates not unfairly some of the consequences of attempted repression, and effectively portrays the prejudicial effect it had upon the manners and morals of men who believed themselves to be treated unjustly and harshly, and who were thus tempred to break the law. "The King of Borva" is represented as speaking thus:—"Tarbert?" said Mr Mackenzie; "you wass wanting to know about Tarbert? Ah, well, it is getting to be a better place now, but a year or two ago it was ferry like hell. Oh, yes, it wass, Shiela, so you need not say anything. And this wass the way of it, Mr Lavender, that the trawling was not made legal then;

and the men, they were just like teffles, with the swearing, and the drinking, and the quarrelling going on; and if you went into the harbour in the open day, you would find them drunk and fighting, and some of them with blood on their faces, for it wass a ferry wild time. It wass many a one will say that the Tarbert men would run down the police-boat some dark night. And what wass the use of catching the trawlers now and again, and taking their boats and their nets to be sold at Greenock, when they would go themselves over to Greenock to the auction and buy them back? Oh it wass a great deal of money they made then—I hef heard of a crew of eight men getting £30 each man in the course of one night, and that not seldom mirover."

"But why didn't the Government put it down?" Lavender asked.

A FAVOURING BREEZE.

"Well, you see, Mackenzie answered, with the air of a man acquainted with the difficulties of ruling; "you see that it wass not quite sure that the trawling did much harm to the fishing. And the *Juckal*—that wass the Government steamer—she wass not much good in getting the better of the Tarbert men, who are ferry strong with their boats in the rowing, and are very cunning besides. For the buying boats they would go out to sea; and take the herring there; and then the trawlers they would sink their nets and come home in the morning as if they had not caught one fish, although the boat would be white with the scales of the herring. And what is more, sir, the Government knew ferry well that if trawling wass put down then, there would be a ferry good many murders; for the Tarbert men, when they came home to drink whisky, and wash the whisky down with porter, they were ready to fight anybody."

"It must be a delightful place to live in," Lavender said.

"Oh, but it is ferry different now," Mackenzie continued, "ferry different. The men they are nearly all Good Templars now, and there is no drinking whatever, and there is reading-rooms and such things, and the place is ferry quiet and respectable. . . . I can say for them, Mr Lavender, that there is no better fishermen on the coast. They are ferry fine tall men; and they are ferry well dressed in their blue clothes; and they are manly fellows, whether they are drunk or whether they are sober. Now look at this, sir, that in the worst of weather they will neffer tek whisky with them when they go out to sea at night, for they think it is cowardly. And they are ferry fine fellows and gentlemanly in their ways, and they are ferry good-natured to strangers."

The novelist's description of those warlike days will stand true for all time as a realistic picture of a period which was full of excitement to a generation which is speedily passing away. Nor is his testimony less true as to the unfailing courtesy and gentlemanly bearing of the fishermen of Tarbert towards the stranger within their gates, for many a visitor has experienced their friendship and kindly attention, and has had his holiday brightened thereby.

"Oh bonnie was my boatie
Afloat upon the bay."

In the prosecution of fishing by trawl or seine-net, the type of boat employed on Loch Fyne is a trim, brightly-varnished, four-oared skiff, carrying a jib and lugsail. At the period of which the novelist writes, the Tarbert skiff was a comparatively light, open boat of 23 feet keel, easily rowed, and costing, all-found, only about £19. To shelter the men during the day, when circumstances made it necessary for them to be from home throughout the week, they latterly carried tents on board, which they pitched by the shore in some sheltered nook or bay.

A few years' experience of tent life and of the hardships which it entailed, led to the gradual development of the skiff up to its present proportions. The improved and enlarged boat of thirty years ago, with a small forward deck, cost £40, and in it the fishermen contrived to live when from home, using a tarpaulin to cover in the midship portion. Ten years later the skiff measured 25 feet keel and 9 feet beam, costing, when ready for sea, £72.

HOLIDAYING SATURDAY AFTERNOON.

The boat of the present day is a roomy and able craft, and affords a measure of comfort to the men which was undreamt of by their forefathers. Its dimensions are 26 feet keel, 36 feet overall, and 10 feet beam; and its cost is, when clinker built, £115, and when carvel built, £150.

The number of such boats hailing from Tarbert is 80, and as each boat is manned by a crew of four men (all of them joint and equal owners), the number of trawl fishermen resident in the village and its immediate neighbourhood is 320. Most of the skiffs are built in the yards of the village, of which there are four, and when times are good their construction gives life to a useful and interesting industry, which includes also yacht, motor-launch, and small-boat building.

"Hò mo bhàta laghach,
S'tu mo bhàta grinn;
Mo bhàta boidheach laghach,
Thogadh taobh Loch Fin."

An interesting development in the evolution of the trawling skiff has taken shape within recent months, by the introduction into several Campbeltown skiffs of motors for propulsion. These motors generate a speed of about five knots. At present the idea is in the experimental stage, but should the motors prove satisfactory in other regards, we may look to their universal adoption, as they will render the fishers in large measure independent of weather conditions.

The Trawl Net.

During the period with which we are now dealing, the dimensions of the trawl net have increased in keeping with the increased size of the boat. Twenty years ago a trawl net measured 170 yards in length, and at its centre or bag, about 38 yards in depth. Its cost, when made up, and complete with all the necessary ropes, was £34. The net in use at the present day costs £38, and is 290 yards long and 40 yards deep.

The setting up of a trawl net demands a considerable amount of skill on the part of the fishermen. Form and strength are given to it by the attachment of ropes along the top and bottom—the back and sole, and its centre takes the shape of a great bag for the reception of the entrapped herring. A multitude of corks arranged along the back-rope support the latter on the surface of the water. To each end of the net a bridle of rope is affixed, and to these bridles "sweep" ropes are attached which, in working, are used for drawing the net through the water and towards the boats. In earlier times (forty years ago) a stout piece of wood at each end took the place of the present rope bridles.

"Take your seat beside the window;
There you'll see the breezy bay,
And the brown sails of the fishers
Dipping in the white sea-spray."

Whether witnessed from the window looking out upon the loch, from the grassy Castle Hill, or from the old gray rocks which guard the bay, few sights on the Scottish coasts are so interesting as is the graceful procession of the fishing fleet on a summer afternoon from the land-locked harbour of Tarbert. To visitors it is an ever-recurring source of interest and delight. As the dark brown wings are hoisted to the breeze, skiff follows skiff in rapid succession, threading their way through the narrow channels, and passing on the right the "Perch," the old-time familiar sea-mark which stands sentry among the waves and guards the gateway. In a few minutes the procession is seen to open fan-like on the wide expanse of Loch Fyne. The destination of each pair (for in trawling, two boats work in concert throughout the season) is determined by a variety of circumstances—the direction of the wind, the character of the weather, or current reports as to the presence of herring in certain parts of the Loch or in neighbouring waters.

YACHT-SLIP AND BOAT-BUILDING YARD.

A night spent with the trawlers (and many visitors have had the good fortune to experience the novelty) carries with it a charm which long lingers in the memory; for fishing by trawl, when herring are plentiful, and the weather fine, is not only interesting but intensely exciting.

Arrived in the neighbourhood of their chosen fishing ground, the crews await in their several ways the coming of the evening hour. As they wait, they watch and they listen for signs of the presence of their prey. The spouting of the herring-whale, the gambols of the frolicsome porpoise, the descent of the shooting solan—all of them indications of the presence of herring—are not lost on the eager fishers, and in the calm of the summer twilight no sound is so welcome as the "plop" of the "playing" herring, which often reveals the presence of millions of its kind, so markedly gregarious is the herring tribe.

As darkness closes in, and the boats move about under sail or oar, keen eyes peer into the deep, watching intently for the fiery trail of the herring, as, frightened by some sudden noise, they rush through the phosphorescent glistening sea. "The sea," says an old writer, "hath its stars no less than the sky," and those myriad light-bearers, little specks of living jelly, which make the ocean glow with their strange, uncanny light, are the fisher's friends and allies, often revealing to him the eagerly longed for spoil.

At such a time, and in the restful calm of a summer night, the eerie silences, the ghost-like flitting of skiff or steamer over the "burning" (*losgudh*) waters, the rustling overhead of the hovering, companionable gulls, the plowter of the sea at the bow, the twinkling masthead lights of rival steamers, or the gleam of a flaring flambeau from a fortunate trawler arouse feelings, and create impressions, even in the most dull-minded, which are not easily effaced. But the excitement attending the prospective capture of a heavy haul effectually banishes, for the time being, all mooning or poetic sentiment, and in an instant all hands are alert and active.

How the Tarbert Trawlers Fish.

The method of procedure in trawling is as follows: From one of the two boats which act together a rope, many fathoms in length, is passed to the crew of the other boat, by whom it is speedily fastened to one end of the net. While the former boat, meantime, remains stationary, the latter, under sail or oar, proceeds to shoot the net in the form of a semi-circle. When the net is all into the water, it is followed by a rope equal in length to that held by the consort, both boats the while sailing or pulling to the shore in parallel lines till they cast their anchors in shallow water. And now begins a long and a strong pull, the crew of each boat dragging the net until its ends are brought within twenty fathoms of the boats. Both ropes are now taken in charge by the crew which shot the net, and by them the trawl is gradually dragged on board, while the consort, passing round to the centre of the loop, supports the back-rope to prevent the fish leaping out as they are being lifted in baskets from the bag of the net. Soon the crews may be knee deep in the most beautiful inhabitants of the waters, for such is the silvery herring when freshly removed from its native element.

A PLEASING TARBERT SPECTACLE.

The catches sometimes secured by this method of fishing are enormous. Only a few seasons ago, one crew, after summoning to its aid half-a-dozen extra boats, sent to market as the result of one haul about 350,000 herring, or one each for half of the population of Glasgow! It is the knowledge of the unfailing ocurrence of good seasons after times of continued disappointment that makes hope ever burn brightly in the breast of the Tarbert fisherman. A single season, or even a single night, may raise him from poverty to comparative affluence, and he holds by his trawl and continues to hope.

Another method of fishing by trawl-net, known as "ringing," has been thus graphically described by one who writes from an intimate knowledge of the procedure. In the quotation the modern method of disposing of the fish after capture is also interestingly described. Morning was approaching, but as yet no success had come to the weary fishers, "I was on the point of crawling in by the fire, out of the chill dawn," says the writer, "when a ripple on the elsewhere unwrinkled surface of the water just caught my eye. It was a herring taking water, and in a moment it flashed in silver, turned in the air, and took the water with a fine rich 'plop.'

" 'Not a bloomin' star—an' black,' said one; for the sky was now overcast. Pipes were smothered out, and a few ringing orders went about, but the men knew their work. The haliards whirred in the blocks, and the sail came rattling home as the sistership drew in, took the rope-end of the trawl, and paid the trawl away. In a few minutes both boats were sweeping in a circle, and one of them casting a trawl as she went, while the other end was made fast to the neighbouring boat, and a dark circular patch of water was enclosed in a long line of corks, with here and there a buoy. The net was shot. Every noise in the stillness seemed to me louder than it was, and the nervous strain made it impossible for me to keep still. The crisp air was making me shiver in any case, but the thought of the unseen millions (perhaps) of fish that might be swimming in captivity in the shadowy waters of that circle—how near, how far away, you cannot tell—wrought me to an excitement. There is just the critical point when the trawl is out and about to he hauled again. Somehow I think the men take hold of the rope as if to divine by an electric current through it whether the bag is bursting full, or whether the net be empty. They began hauling, and meshed herrings glittered, struggling as they left the sea. The men would promise nothing as yet. Then someone spat out an oath, and said the trawl was going fast on bad ground. I held my peace, for when the air is vexed with profanity, and men sorely tried at their business, least said, best. They swore tumultuously, calling on their sea-deities, on each other, and on me, to witness how time and again these rocks despoiled them. But on a sudden the good trawl seemed to clear itself, and came slipping in handsomely, and profanity ceased. Excitement was sifting into my blood as I saw the net smeared with silver, and flashing white as it rose out of the sea, and one at last put me out of suspense. 'By jove, boys, but we have a poultice o' them.' The two boats drew together as the circle lessened, and soon seven men were basketing fine big herring from the net to the boat. Higher rose the fish in the boat, and lower she settled, till she floated a foot only out of the water.

"I leaped to the torch, and in a wink had it flaring. On the instant, from every point of the compass, red and green lights were bearing down on us, and one steamer came racing up near enough to give me sickly visions of being run down. Punts came dancing over the waves to us, and a legion of buyers swarmed on board, for the night's fishing was poor among the fleet.

MENDING NETS AT THE OLD BATTERY.

"All gazed longingly on the fish, but for a space none spoke. At last 15s. a basket was offered, and so it rose till but two held the field—19s., 19s. 6d. 'Gi'es a clean not (*i.e.*, note) an' ye'll get them.' 'All right; if ye put them aboard in half-an-hour,' and the lucky buyer muttered something about catching a train as he scurried back to his steamer. An hour later, 240 baskets were stowed aboard, and we set our faces home on the heels of a dawn-wind."

This market on the open sea is a striking evidence of the enterprise of the age. Thirty years ago it was almost unknown. Up till about that period, all the herring caught in the neighbourhood of Tarbert were sold at Tarbert quay for conveyance by goods steamer to Glasgow, where they were disposed of as fresh herring late that night or early next day; or were retained at the quay, or in vessels in the harbour, in order to be cured.

Now all is changed, and with it has departed much of the old bustle and stir of Tarbert quay and bay. But it is well, for the new method is much more convenient for fisher and buyer. Nor is the competition on the fishing ground less keen, as a rule, than under former conditions, for the flaring flambeau brings the buying steamers around the fortunate boats like moths round a candle, and the huckstering is carried on with sharpness and eagerness, amid abundance of good-humoured chaff and genial banter, not unmixed, occasionally, with stinging sarcasm.

The new method is also much more expeditious than the old, and therein lies its chief advantage. A wider market for fresh herring is now commanded, while, incredible though it may seem, the consumer in Glasgow and its neighbourhood may breakfast off herring that four hours earlier were disporting themselves in the blue waters of Loch Fyne!

This marketing on the highway of the sea is essentially a cash trade. No sooner are the boxes packed and counted than the equivalent in bank notes, be it much or little, is passed to the fisherman who acts as treasurer. On each Saturday afternoon a distribution of the profits is made—share and share alike—after a portion has been set aside to meet or to reduce the company's liabilities.

There is, undoubtedly, much to be said (in theory at any rate) for this community of interest, for each has equal stimulus to diligent and persevering effort. It is a form of practical socialism. The stimulus, however, it is not difficult to see, will not always act with equal force on every member of the crew, with the result that the more energetic and persevering and adventurous men will often find their desires and efforts frustrated by the less intelligent and less pushful.

The Future of the Loch Fyne Fishing.

The herring, the real king of fishes, has many enemies—enemies of the air, of the sea, and of the land—but still their number seems to be undiminished; and it is questionable if these enemies account, to any marked degree, for the hard times which the fishers have periodically to endure.

Statistics go to prove that good years and bad years run in groups, and the recent series of bad years was almost exactly paralleled thirty-two years ago. It is comforting to reflect that, unsatisfactory though recent seasons have been, the amount of herring caught within the Loch Fyne and Campbeltown districts during the past twenty-six years is well-nigh double the amount landed during the immediately preceding twenty-six years.

DRIFTING OUT.

Such facts lead many to argue that the destruction effected by men, and fish, and birds, great though it be, is negligible, and that men are justified in taking herring when, and where, and how they may. It may be so. So far as the efforts of man are concerned, Professor McIntosh, of St. Andrews, asserts that "it has not been proved that our seas have been depleted of food-fishes to a dangerous extent by man," and that "the sea can hold its own even against human cupidity." A herring that weighs six or seven ounces contains, on an average, thirty thousand eggs; and Buffon calculated that if a single pair of herrings could be left to breed and multiply undisturbed for a period of twenty years, they would yield a quantity of fish equal in bulk to the entire substance of the globe!

These, and other facts that might be adduced, are fitted to inspire men with hope, even in the worst of times, and it is not difficult to believe that, ere long, the Golden Year will again come round. Its coming should, however, be hastened by all possible means, for the industry— one of our greatest national assets—is well worth caring for. Only last year there were caught within the British Seas 3,000,000 crans (400,000 tons) of herring, providing a vast store of wholesome and nourishing food, of a monetary value of £2,250,000 To know the way of the fish in the sea is difficult, and there is at present little room for the holding of strong opinions regarding the habits of the herring, but these are being closely investigated by leading scientists, and it is probable that ere many years have fled, the vagaries of the "poor man's fish" will be better understood, and the welfare of the hardy toilers of the deep be more assured.

PASSING THE ISLAND.

In this connection, and on account of the succession of bad seasons which the fishermen of Loch Fyne have recently experienced, fishing on the Ballantrae spawning banks between January 15th and March 31st has been prohibited during the past six years, while from May 16th of the present year, all beam or otter trawling in the Firth of Clyde is to cease. The effect of these restrictions is being carefully studied by the scientific staff of the Fishery Board; and other questions, such as the proposed rescinding of the restriction on daylight fishing in June, the inclusion of the Sound of Kilbrannan within the protected area during the spring spawning season, and the influence upon the herring of torpedo-firing in the Firth, are receiving the anxious consideration of the Board.

IN THE OUTER HARBOUR.

So far as Loch Fyne is concerned, there is little hope of the habits of the herring and its life-history receiving that thorough study which is so necessary and so desirable until a well-equipped marine laboratory is established at a convenient centre—such as Tarbert —and a steamer is placed at the disposal of the Fishery Board. Many questions, such as the circumstances which govern the increase and decrease of the innumerable organisms which constitute the food of the herring—the flow of the currents; the temperature of the sea; its saltness—the periods of spawning; the situation of the spawning banks; the difference (if any) between spring spawners and autumn spawners; the value of "spawny" herring as a human food; the number of years which herring take to come to maturity, and whether or not the

Firth of Clyde is a self-contained area for herrings, might then be settled beyond cavil. These are fundamental questions, and they call for definite scientific answers. Satisfactory legislation cannot be framed on ideas which are speculative rather than informed, and the Fishery Board do well to refrain from the enforcement of further restrictive measures until the points in dispute are scientifically determined, or the fishermen are themselves practically agreed in their attitude towards them.

FOR CHILD AND WIFE.

Out from the harbour, and over the wave,
　The trim skiff bounds like a thing of life,
And blue-clad fishermen, hardy and brave,
Heed not the winds as they bluster and rave,
　For their thoughts are at home with child and wife,

And they dream of a silvery prize from the sea,
　As the proud skiff buffets the dark Loch Fyne;
And they dream of the hearths that shall gladdened be
When the teeming wave yields its treasures free,
　And no more shall the hungry bairnies pine.

But the sea is cruel, and guards its store
　With more than a miser's jealous care;
And the night steals down on Kilbrannan's shore,
While the lightnings flash and the hurricanes roar,
　And the heart is filled with a dull despair.

Then the winds are hushed, and keen eyes peer
　In the glowing depths of the "burning" sea;
And the old men dream of the Golden Year
As they pray to the God whom they worship and fear;
　But the Heavens are deaf to the bairnies' plea.

Thus the weeks and the months pass drearily by,
　Till the hearth is cold and the board is bare;
And strong men mutter a curse or a sigh,
And women sit gloomy with tear-dimmed eye,
　And the Heavens are deaf to the bairnies' prayer.

Ah! 'twas ever thus with the fickle sea.
　But the Golden Year is ever nigh;
And the morn awakes, and the shadows flee,
And the women forget their misery,
　For the good God heard the bairnies' cry.

*"I ever loved our earth, and still
I love its scaurs and brooks and braes."*

Much, as we have seen, has been done in recent years to add to the attractiveness of Tarbert as a seaside resort; but, for many people, its principal charm will still be found in its picturesque natural features, its historic associations, its antiquarian remains, the freedom of its heathery hills, the variety of its walks and drives, its safe boating, and its unsophisticated fisher-life. Several of Scotland's most famous modern painters have here found their happiest subjects.

FROM THE NORTH-EAST.

Lovers of the things of old will take an early opportunity of climbing the castle hill, and wandering among the ruins of the old gray storied pile. Guide book in hand, they will have little difficulty in tracing the foundations of the greater part of the castle of Bruce, which in its day was such an important stronghold, and the scene of many a court and lordly revel. Antiquarians will join with us in hoping that this interesting historic ruin will at an early date come under the care of the recently appointed Royal Commission, and that effective measures will soon be taken for its preservation.

Visitors who value the privilege of roaming over the hillsides and escaping from the dusty highway, will heartily appreciate the freedom that is here enjoyed. From Maoldarach's grassy height on the east, the heathy hill of Roebuck, which overlooks the village from the north, and from many another colgn of vantage on the circling hills they will be charmed with the beauty and extent of the view.

Pedestrians who do not fear a climb of a much

more formidable character, providing a yet more ample reward, cannot do better than essay the mountain slope of Sliabh Gaoil. The approach is up the hillside, west of Ashens House, and on past the north end of Loch-a-Chaoran, till the highest point is reached. Sliabh Gaoil is a range of mountains rather than an individual hill. It occupies the space between Loch Fyne and Loch Caolisport, and extends south-west from the neighbourhood of Inverneil, a distance of twelve miles. From its highest peak—1840 feet—"it commands one of the most extensive, varied, and grandly picturesque views in Great Britain." West Loch Tarbert, Loch Caolisport, Gigha, Islay, Jura, Scarba, Mull, Arran, the north of Ireland, Loch Fyne, Ben Cruachan, Ben Lomond, many of the mountains of Perthshire, the Kyles of Bute, and the mouth of the Clyde are all distinctly visible under favourable weather conditions. An excursion to Sliabh Gaoil will richly reward the traveller.

Through Glenralloch and round Roebuck Hill.

This is a favourite circular walk of three and a-half miles. It is best entered upon from the Ardrishaig road. Rounding the east end of Roebuck, the road by a quick descent strikes into the glen at a distance of one and a-half miles from the village. On both hands the hillsides are beautiful. A walk of a few hundred yards brings the traveller to the highest point in the glen, from which, looking backward, picturesque glimpses are had of Loch Fyne and the hills of Cowal.

As we descend the solitary glen, West Loch Tarbert, fringed with sylvan greenery, stretches away before us, placid and glistening and beautiful. As the glen opens out towards the loch, the farmhouse of Glenralloch, surrounded by sheltering trees, is passed on a little eminence on the right. A small loch, known as the "Lily Loch," from the presence of water lilies on its surface, is easily reached after a tew minutes' walk over the hill immediately behind the farmhouse. Cultivated fields and stretches of woodland soften and beautify the landscape on either hand as the road approaches the head of the loch. Holding by the left, we skirt the base of Roebuck,

cross the head of the loch, and join the Tarbert and Campbeltown
road at a distance of about three-quarters of a mile from Tarbert, and
thus complete a favourite afternoon walk.

To Ardrishaig.

The Ardrishaig road, over the beginning of which we have been
travelling on our excursion to Sliabh Gaoil and our walk through
Glenralloch, looks down on Tarbert from the north. As we ascend
the ridge, a charming little panorama is disclosed—the village circling
round the rocky bay, the peaceful harbour embraced by its hills, and
guarded by its island, and presiding over all the old gray castle with
its stern back-ground of heathery hills.

> "And now and then comes like a dream
> A white-sailed yacht into the bay."

PANORAMIC VIEW FROM BRUACHNASUGH.

At a distance of somewhat less than a mile from the village is the
gateway to the policies of Stonefield House, the residence of C. G.
P. Campbell, Esq., Laird of Tarbert. Stonefield House, which stands
on a small plateau overlooking Loch Fyne, occupies one of the most
picturesque sites imaginable. The approach is along a winding avenue,
beautifully varied in character, and over a lofty ivy-covered bridge,
which spans a romantic gully, through which flows an impetuous
rivulet. Indigenous plants in great variety find a congenial home on

the steep banks of the stream, and in the neighborhood of the house, attesting the mildness of this beautiful sheltered spot.

Retracing our steps to the lodge gateway, we proceed on our journey towards Ardrishaig. From the lodge the road strikes somewhat more inland, till it descends into Glenralloch. On the right, near the point of junction with the Glenralloch road, is the steading of Stonefield home-farm, and on the left the house attached to the large sheep-farm of Ashens. A little farther along, and through a break in the wood on the right, a glimpse of Stonefield House is obtained.

A rugged yet beautiful part of the way is now entered upon, and for a mile and a-half or so the road stretches along an elevated plateau, by broken woodland and by ferny brake, till it quickly descends to the sea-level at the north lodge of Stonefield policies, and in the neighbourhood of Maol-Mor, the property of Edward Aitken, Esq. Looking toward the south, the green peninsula of Barmore is seen projecting its bulky form out into the loch, its narrow isthmus, consisting, as it does, of a tiny thread of green, constituting it one of the most perfect examples of a peninsula to be found anywhere. Opposite, on the Cowal coast, is Ardmarnock House, the residence of Mrs D. N. Nicol, widow of the late esteemed member for the county. Somewhat farther north is the large bay of Kilfinnan, while still further up the Cowal coast the point (or spit) of Otter juts far into the loch, and marks the entrance to Upper Loch Fyne.

From Maol-Mor onward to Ardrishaig, the road closely skirts the water. At a distance of five miles from Tarbert the House of Erines (Norse—*Eyrr*, a gravelly beach), is passed, the property of Sir John Denison Pender, K.C.M.G. From 1856 to 1859 lead mines were worked among the hills on the estate of Erines, but the metal was not obtained in paying quantities. A year ago men's hearts were cheered by the discovery of gold on the hillside, three miles nearer Ardrishaig, but in this matter also expectations remain up to this time unrealised.

Hereabout the rock and shore scenery is very fine, and the precipitous hillsides, craggy and rugged in no ordinary degree, are richly clad in a mantle of brushwood and sturdy fern. In the neighbourhood of Ardteligan (6 ½ miles) was fought, in all probability, a battle, which is recorded under date 574 in the *Annals of Ulster* and in the *Annals of Tighernac*. In the latter *Annals* it is called the Battle of Delgon, and the combatants were the Scots of Dalriada and (probably) the Picts. In the *mêlée*, Duncan, son of the Scots King, Conall, was slain, together with "many others of the tribe of Gabhran," that tribe which inhabited Kintyre and Knapdale.

Beyond Ardteligan is the bold, bare headland of Maol-Dubh (Black Headland.) As we pursue our way towards our journey's end, Tigh-an-Droighnein Bay, Stronachullin, Bay-an-Tailleir, and the ruined church of Inverneil (8 ½ miles) are successively passed on the right. On the left, at some distance off the road, is Inverneil House, while a little farther along, on the sea-ward side, are Brenfield Bay and Point. In the neighbourhood of Ardrishaig (11 ½ miles) the scenery takes on a softer character, and the road is lined with many handsome villas which tell of comfort and elegance. This walk by the noble, far-stretching Loch Fyne is perhaps the most beautiful in the neighbourhood, and has few equals throughout the length and breadth of Scotland.

THE "PIONEER" AT THE WEST PIER.

To Clachan.

Historic as a national highway to and from the Western Isles, the western exit from Tarbert over the narrow isthmus leads, in these modern days, in three directions:—

(1) To Clachan and Campbeltown.

(2) To Skipness and Carradale.

(3) To Kilberry and Ormsary.

We shall, in turn, traverse a few miles of these roads, and note points of interest as we go.

The construction of the outer pier, to which reference has already been made, added greatly to the importance of Tarbert as a transit centre. It led, more particularly, to the opening up of the peninsula, and to improved communication with the old home of the Lords of the Isles. The former was effected by the substitution, in the year 1866, of the present mail and passenger coach for the mail-gig, by which, for generations, letters had been conveyed to and from Campbeltown and the hamlets *en route*.

In consequence of increased vehicular traffic resulting from these and other developments, the narrow by-way leading from West Tarbert to the "Islay Pier" was in 1868 re-made, considerably widened, and carried, as at present, round the Carrick till it joined the high road on the margin of Eascairt Bay. On the completion of this beautiful piece of roadway by the side of the loch, the steep and somewhat dangerous road over the Carrick was closed to general traffic. It may still, however, be traversed on foot, and the walk "round the Carrick," going by the low road and returning by the high road, is always a favourite with visitors. The distance from Tarbert is 4 miles.

As far back as the year 1764 regular communication (wind and weather permitting) was kept up once a week between West Tarbert and Islay by means of a sailing packet. In the summer of 1824 this packet gave place to the first steamer on the route, the *Maid of Islay*, a vessel of 140 tons burthen. Two successors of this pioneer steamer were named the *Islay*—the old and the new. The latter was owned and managed by the late John Ramsay, Esq. of Kildalton.

Up to the year 1877 the sailings were limited to the summer months, and the number of trips to one a week, as a rule. The day of call was Tuesday, but on occasion a call was made on Friday also. Daily sailings were instituted in 1877, and in 1879 the traffic was taken over by David Hutchison & Co., the predecessors of David M'Brayne, Limited.

It is impossible to foretell what the future has in store in the matter of traffic development between the eastern and the western lochs. Time and again, since the days of James Watt and Henry Bell, the narrowness of the isthmus (1600 yards), and its lowness (47 feet above high-water mark), have suggested the cutting of a maritime canal, or the formation of a ship railway, for the convenience of commerce. Unfortunately, as we think, all such schemes have up to this time fallen through; and there seems to be little prospect of any project of this nature being carried out in the future unless its promoters can count on a substantial contribution in aid from the Imperial exchequer.

THE MAN-FACED ROCK.

As we enter on the isthmus-roadway on our excursion to Clachan (the old shrine of St. Colman Ela), the Parish church towers over us on the left, while on the right the manse nestles, sheltered and secluded among its greenery. Close by the manse are the recreation grounds of the village, consisting of bowling-green, tennis-courts, and football field, all of which are largely taken advantage of by visitors. On the left, in the neighbourhood of the old hamlet of Lagluinge, is the Drill Hall and Public Library.

The Western Loch.

Passing the hamlet of Carnban we quickly gain the shores of West Loch Tarbert and the hamlet of the same name. Here, in a building still standing on the right, considerable quantities of whisky were distilled in days gone by. Leaving the old highway over the Carraig on the left, a walk of fully half-a-mile by the side of the beautiful water, and past the "man-faced rock" which overlooks the road, brings us to the west pier, at which the steamer *Pioneer* from Islay makes her daily call. Right opposite the pier is the grassy point of *Abhainn-na-gillean.*

"Bonny West Loch Tarbert," is an arm of the Atlantic measuring about ten miles in length, with a mean breadth of about three-quarters of a mile. On account of the mildness of the climate it is usually frequented in winter by the widgeon and wild swan. Oysters are cultivated on its shores. In the "Old Statistical Account" of 1794 we read that they were then to be had in considerable quantities. They "were sold on the spot at 6d, the hundred, and sent to the markets of Campbeltown and Greenock."

The scenery of West Loch Tarbert, with its "soft outlines and wooded shores," reminds the tourist of Windermere rather than of any other Scottish sea-loch. It is in marked contrast with the stern ruggedness and wildness of its eastern sister, and Lord Teignmouth, who sailed down West Loch Tarbert in 1827, wrote of the two lochs as exhibiting "the contrast of a painting by Claude to one by Salvator Rosa." The scenery of the West Loch he characterises as "beautiful."

MacCulloch's description of the loch and its surroundings, as viewed from the Kintyre highway, is effective and just:—"The navigation of Loch Tarbert is exceedingly beautiful, without being strictly picturesque. The ground is neither high nor bold; but the shores are varied in form and character, often beautifully wooded, and in many places highly cultivated; while a considerable rural population, and some houses of more show and note, give it that dressed and civilised air which is by no means an usual feature in the shores of the Highlands. . . . I know not what Loch Tarbert may be at other times, but when I made its circuit it was with sunrise on one of the loveliest mornings of June. The water was like a mirror, and as the sun reached the dewy birchwoods the air was perfumed by their fragrance, while the warbling of ten thousand thrushes on all sides, with the tinkling sound of the little waves that curled on the shore, and the gentle whispering of the morning air among the trees, rendered it a perfect scene of enchantment." These descriptions will be fully appreciated as we proceed on our journey.

Half-a-mile beyond the pier, Eascairt Bay is reached, sheltered by Eilean-da-Ghallagan, the island of the two little ports or landing places, long associated with the name of the old sea pirate, Alan-nan-Sop. In its neighbourhood, boats trading with the Clyde anchored in earlier times, and found protection from the storms. Dr. Skene, in his "Celtic Scotland," notes that John, Lord of the Isles, dates a charter from "Clandaghallagan" in Knapdale; and, in default of other identification, he accepted a suggestion made to him by the late Mr Hugh McLean of Breaclarach that the place referred to is Eilean-da-Ghallagan, the transcriber mistaking the initial letter E for C. The suggestion seems eminently reasonable.

THE WEST LOCH FROM THE OLD ROAD.

From this point, the fortress-crag of Dunskeig, eight miles distant, is seen away to the south, standing out boldly against the sky. After rounding the bay, a glimpse is had through an open glade on the left of the prettily situated Eascairt House. Close by the house, it may be noted, are five rude stone pillars which are marked on the Ordnance Map as part of a stone circle. The largest of the stones is a "splendid monolith of schistose rock, measuring some 11 feet high, 5 feet broad, and 15 in. in its greatest thickness."

Striking more inland, Corranbuidh, Sunnyside, Woodhouse, and Rhu (3½ miles) are successively passed, the latter an old residence of the younger Stonefields. The plantations hereabout are very extensive, reaching for miles together without a break. They were first planted by the laird of Stonefield, John Campbell, between the years 1830 and 1840; and, by clothing the hillsides, must have contributed much to the beauty of the landscape. To the left of the road, where it turns off sharply above the island-guarded bay of Ceann-na-Craig, is the old burying place of Cladh Bhride, sheltered by a cluster of trees. Here lie buried some members of the Stonefield family. Cladh Bhride was, in early days, one of the five dependent chapelries of Kilcalmonell, and it is at this day the only one that retains any vestiges of a chapel.

Leaving, on the left, the Skipness road, which strikes right across the country to the other side of Kintyre, we reach, at a distance of six miles from Tarbert, the snug village of Whitehouse or Lag-a-Mhuilinn, with its post and telegraph office, its school, its blacksmith's shop, and its sawmill, from which latter the village derives its more poetic Gaelic name.

From Whitehouse on to Clachan, the road is hilly in the extreme, but ample compensation is found in the beauty of the view obtained from the elevated situation. A majestic panorama is spread out before us from those solitary uplands. Loch and island, wooded glade and cultivated slope, backed by far-reaching rounded hills and gray moors, go to the composition of a picture not easily surpassed.

> "Its fields were speckled, its forests green,
> And its lakes were all of the dazzling sheen,
> Like magic mirrors, where slumbering lay
> The sun and the sky and the cloudlet gray."

On leaving Whitehouse, we successively pass on the right hand the farmhouse of Kilchamaig or Kilcharmaig (where at one time there stood a chapel dedicated to St. Cormac, the bold monkish navigator, who sailed into the Arctic Ocean for fourteen days before a south wind), and Gartnagrenach, where "a host of golden daffodils" clothes the fields in the early months of spring.

The Crannogs on Lochan Dughaill.

About a mile farther along, high among the hills, and out of sight of West Loch Tarbert, we approach the bed of an erstwhile moorland loch which, within recent years, has been a centre of much interest to antiquarians. This little loch, known as Lochan Dughaill, is set down on the Ordnance Map as a little sheet of water on the southern side of the highway, measuring 600 yards in length by about 300 yards in breadth, which found an exit into Loch Tarbert.

Following upon unsuccessful attempts to permanently reclaim the land to agriculture made in the years 1807 and 1870, Sir William McKinnon of Balanakill, who in his day did so much for the building up of the British Empire in Africa, accomplished the efficient drainage of the loch in 1890.

THE WEST LOCH FROM EILEAN-DA-GHALLAGAN.

During the operations, certain wooden structures, which had been partially disclosed by the removal of the water, were surmised to be the remains of crannogs or lake dwellings—those primitive erections which the men of earlier times often constructed, and resorted to as places of retreat "in dangerous hour."

Tarbert

In the year 1892, Dr. Robert Munro, F.S.A., with the assistance of the proprietor and several local enthusiasts, set the matter at rest, with results of exceptional importance. Two crannogs were discovered, and one of them was investigated with great thoroughness. In his report, Dr Munro says of it:—"Lochan Dughaill crannog is unique, inasmuch as it is the first in Scotland which has yielded clear evidence as to the kind of dwelling-house erected by the crannog builders. Here it was a large, circular, tent-like structure, 32 feet in diameter, constructed of wood, and supported by one central and some twenty surrounding uprights." This crannog was also singular, inasmuch as it was divided into a *but* and a *ben*. The outer doorway led into the former, and in this was also discovered a hearth resting upon a specially prepared log flooring, formed of the trunks of trees still retaining the bark. The artificial island upon which the house was erected was shown to have been constructed of timbers and brushwood, laid in layers transversely to each other. The whole was surrounded by a stockade of an oval shape, measuring 45 feet from east to west, and 49 feet from north to south. The relics found consist of a flint scraper, a perforated stone disc used probably for twisting the strands of a fisherman's lines, four sharpening stones, five quartz polishers, a portion of a ring bracelet of cannel coal, a jar of glazed earthenware "of rather elegant design," a very small crucible, evidently intended for smelting the rarer metals, and certain bones of the ox, sheep, and deer.

There is nothing to show at what period these interesting structures were erected, but history records that as late as the year 1608, crannogs were being utilised in the Isles as places of strength and places of retreat.

Local tradition tells the following story of the "Dugald" from whom the loch took its name. Several centuries ago, when "King Fingal," Chief of the McDonalds, lived in the Castle of Saddell, a warrior named Dugald Mac Gruamal (the Surly One), who was looked upon as a sort of man-wolf, led a band of men from Ireland to Kintyre, and slew McAlister of Loup. Taking possession of the lands of Loup, he married, against her will, the daughter of McAlister, and took her as captive and wife to live

A Legend of Lochan Dughaill

with him in the Crannog on Lochan Dughaill. No boat was permitted upon the loch but Mac Gruamal's, and his followers residing close by were expected to be prepared to act as a guard on any emergency, or any attempt at rescue.

MAC GRUAMAL ON THE OUT-LOOK.

King Fingal had a natural son known as "Toothed Alexander," whose birth had been delayed, at the suggestion of Fingal's wife, through the incantations of a reputed witch. Hence it came that Alexander was born provided with teeth. One day his father said to him, "I am old, but if you will go and kill that Irishman on the island in the loch, and marry his wife, I will put you in the possession of the lands of Loup." Alexander, must, however, do this by his own skill and courage, and without any help from Fingal.

Alexander agreed to the terms, and ere long found an ally in Mac Gruamal's blacksmith, who was also an Irishman, and lived at Leumna-Muic. In process of time the services of the blacksmith's wife, who was the mid-wife of the district, were required at the Crannog. Upon this probability the allies had been counting, and they had laid their plans accordingly. On the arrival of the messengers from Mac Gruamal, the wily smith, having learned from them to what tree they had tied the boat, said to them, "Sit down a little till my wife makes ready." Meantime the smith and "Toothed Alexander" hastened to the shore of the loch, unfastened the boat, and hurried off to the island. Realising that it was on no peaceful errand they had come, the powerful Mac Gruamal attacked Alexander furiously, and got him under. But the smith, knowing full well that his time of reckoning would assuredly come when Alexander was despatched, came to the help of the latter, and striking Mac Gruamal from behind with his sword, slew him instantly.

In process of time Alexander married the widow, but not before he had complied with three requests (upon which she had insisted)—to build a church between two streams, a mill between two hills, and a house between two woods. They lived thereafter, possessors of Loup—so runs the tale.

The Forts on Dunskeig.

A visit to the fortified hill of Dunskeig, 2 miles beyond Lochan Dughaill, gives the traveller still more fully to realise that Tarbert and its neighbourhood is no less rich in remains interesting to the antiquarian than we have seen it to be in matters of interest to the historian. The hill of Dunskeig is "the most striking natural feature in West Kintyre." Rising sheer up from the shore to a height of 300 feet, it presents from the water a singularly bold aspect, and stands at the mouth of the loch, guarding it, sentinel-wise, on the Kintyre coast, as the headland of Ardpatrick on the opposite shore guards it from the Knapdale side. Its commanding position gave Dunskeig exceptional importance in times of sturt and strife, and its summit was for centuries occupied by places of defence, which were, doubtless, often coveted by contending parties

The top of Dunskeig is somewhat oval in shape, and bears at each end of its long diameter, which runs east and west, the remains of an ancient fort. One, the eastmost, was a circular building of dry stones, portions of which still remain breast high. The entrance, 4 feet 6 inches wide, was on the landward side, and was constructed of the largest blocks. The walls were of great thickness, but are not of the broch type, as they show no evidences of recesses, side chambers, or stairs, as brochs invariably do.

FROM THE CARRAIG ROAD.

More interesting still is the second fort, which belonged to the vitrified type, and overlooks the most precipitous part of the hill. It crowns the Dun on its western brow, at a distance of 50 yards from the first fort. Oval in shape, it measured 26 paces from east to west, and 18 paces from north to south. Vitrifaction, in this example, has evidently been continuous all round. A comparatively small portion of the walls remains, but what there is shows calcined masses of grotesque form, the result of fusion under intense heat. The object of the vitrifaction has evidently been the binding of the walls together in the absence of mortar.

These forts we need not suppose to have been regularly occupied. They were outposts in times of danger, and it is probable that, when they were utilised, they enclosed rude huts of wattle and turf, for the temporary accommodation of the defenders.

The view from the summit of Dunskeig is often exquisitely beautiful. Seaward, the eye scans the islands of Gigba, Cara, Islay, and Jura; away to the north and west are the rolling moorlands and rounded hills of Knapdale; southward Arran towers over the mountains of Kintyre; while, as if at our feet, lies the loch, reaching far inland—quiet, restful, beautiful.

> "O marvel not they love the land
>   Who watch its changeful hills and skies,
> For in its desolation grand,
>   A charm of 'wildr'ing beauty lies."

The Clachan of Kilcalmonell.

A walk of little more than a mile from the summit of Dunskeig brings us down by a quick descent to the pretty little village of Clachan, cosily and picturesquely situated at the entrance of a small glen. At the termination of this glen stands Balanakill House, the residence of John McKinnon, Esq., proprietor of the lands around. Like all *Clachans*, the village has its burn and stepping stones (the name is derived from this circumstance), and the old village, with its church and churchyard, occupied the banks of the stream. Smart, modern cottages, appealing to the summer visitor, now line the highway.

Nothing remains of the original church of the parish, which was dedicated to St. Colman Ela, founder of Muckamore, in Antrim. It is surmised that the site of this ancient shrine was farther up the stream, on a rugged knoll called Bal-na-heglish (the Kirk-toon), on Pont and Bleau's map, and known to the villagers as Shean-na-kill, the ancient cell or church. Traces of an old burying ground exist in the neighbourhood.

St. Colman, from whom the parish of Kilcalmonell (or "Sgire Chalmaineala," as it is called in the district) received its name, derived his surname of Ela or Eala, from a stream of that name in King's County, Ireland. He was a contemporary of St. Columba, and, like him, claimed descent from Niall of the Nine Hostages. According to Tighernac, he was born in Tyrone, in the year 555 and he is referred to on several occasions in Adamnan's "Life of St. Columba."

The present Parish Church, plain and unadorned, was built in the year 1760. In the churchyard will be found "some rude slab carvings of a curious and distinctive type." These seem to have been appropriated, as was not unusual in bygone days, by the old chiefs of the district, the McAlisters of Loupe. One of the stones bears the following inscription:—

"This is the burial place of Ronald McAlister of Dun [skeig] 1707."

Three other stones of the more ornate later mediæval type will also claim the attention of the antiquary. The graceful artwork on these stones is fast becoming obliterated as the result of exposure and neglect. Some day men will lament the indifference which has permitted these and similar treasures of native art to decay and disappear.

In addition to its Parish Church, Clachan possesses an elegant Free Church, the gift of the late Sir William McKinnon. It is also provided with a school, a comfortable inn, and a postal and telegraph office, and is in daily communication with Tarbert by the Tarbert and Campbeltown coach.

WELCOMING THE HERO OF MAFEKING.

To Skipness.

At Kennacraig on the Campbeltown road, five miles from Tarbert, the road to Skipness branches off sharply to the left, and, striking over the upland moor, runs across Kintyre. On the right, on grounds associated with an early home of the Stonefields, stands the mansion-house of Glenreasdell, built in 1905 by the proprietor, P. Jeffrey Mackie, Esq.

All is silence on those lonely moors.

> "There is no voice but the rushing rills,
>   And creak of frightened peewit's wing,
> And bleat of young lambs on the hills,
> Heard only when a silence fills
>   The soul, and all the space of things."

As the higher levels are reached and we glance behind, picturesque glimpses are obtained of West Loch Tarbert and the hills of Knapdale, while gradually in front of us the grand peaks of Arran loom into view.

Passing Glenreasdell Mains on the left, the road quickly descends to sea-level. In the immediate foreground are Claonaig valley and bay, with the parish church on the left bank of Claonaig river, and in a field on the left of the road may be seen the remains of a stone-circle. As in so many other instances throughout Scotland, the stones were, some time ago, appropriated by a farmer for the building of fences. About the centre of the circle may, however, still be seen an open grave cist some 3 feet square, formed of large flagstones set on edge. Surface indications point to the presence of other cists close by, and there can be little doubt that the circumscribed area was an ancient cemetery. Leaving the point of junction with the Crossaig and Carradale road on the right, we proceed on our way towards Skipness (14 miles) by the new road, skirting as we go the rippling waters of the Sound. Right across is the entrance to Lochranza, and away to the east the low-lying island of Bute.

The village of Skipness (*Norse*, Ship-point) is an attractive little place, with the handsome residence of the proprietor, R. C. Graham, Esq., in its immediate neighbourhood. A little pebbled creek in the beautiful, shingly bay is traditionally associated with St. Brendan or St. Brannan, who, probably, often landed there in his journeyings between Bute and Kintyre. Skipness pier, which was erected at a cost of £3000, is situated at about two miles to the north-east.

To the antiquarian, the leading attraction will be the old Castle, which is still in a wonderfully good state of preservation. It is an imposing structure, and of high antiquity. It forms a square with an inner court. "The outer wall measures 7 feet in thickness, is 33 feet high, and 450 feet in circumference. Flanking its eastern side is a small central tower, while of two projecting towers, one at the south-east, and one at the north-east corner, the former was known as Tur an t'sagairt (the priest's tower), while the latter was evidently the keep of the Castle."

Skipness is provided with a postal and telegraph office, and there is an inn at Claonaig.

IN HOLIDAY HOUR.

To Kilberry.

At a distance of about three-quarters of a mile from Tarbert, the road to Kilberry strikes off sharply across the head of West Loch Tarbert, and we enter upon the district of Knapdale (hill and dale). As we cross the isthmus, Glenakill House, sheltered and snug, is observed on the right, commanding a very fine view of the Loch. In olden times there was a burying ground in Glenakill, and a story is told regarding it. About the early part of the eighteenth century a family, who farmed the adjoining ground, thinking they might as well make use of the disused burying-ground and include it in their farm, demolished the wall and removed the tombstones.

This family comprised seven sturdy brothers, all of whom, so runs the story, soon took to a reckless mode of living, went from bad to worse, and died prematurely — a manifest judgment for their sacrilege!

Ere the road turns down by the side of the loch, we cross a pleasant little stream issuing from Glenralloch. Its banks are richly dowered with trees, and the sides of the glen are soft and fair. At the turn of the road is the old cottage of Lochend, which for so long was used as a school, taught by Mr Ronald McAlister. Passing Dubhcladach, an easily traversed road is covered, till presently we reach a fine stream called Abhainn-nan-Gillean (the young men's river), which rushes down its shady glen, and past the old saw-mill, onwards to the sea. The name of the river is thus traditionally derived:—On a certain occasion, five brothers of the name of Campbell were journeying on foot along the shores of the West Loch. On the way they were met by an old woman who was noted for the power of her evil wishes. Having in some way incurred her displeasure, the young men were informed by the old woman that they would never reach the end of their journey. Accordingly, as they were crossing this stream, which was not then bridged over, they one after another slipped from the stepping stones into the rushing waters, and were drowned.

We are now upon the Kintarbert estate, the property of Colonel John McLeod, of Saddell and Kintarbert. Immediately upon crossing the bridge, the road strikes uphill, winding for a time by the side of the woody glen, till soon we are a considerable height above the loch, and on the solitary moorland.

Passing what was once the thriving hamlet of Baraneillan, and the lonely farm-house of Achilach, the road winds down the steep brae of Torr-an-Tuirc to the side of the Loch. On either hand it is bordered by graceful copses, while on the right is the beautifully wooded hill of Craig (the property of John Campbell, Esq. of Kilberry) looking down upon the loch. As we move along, the precipitous rock of Dunmore with its renovated keep, and the lonely churchyard of Kilnaish claim attention.

Dunmore is the property of Evan Campbell Fraser, Esq. On the left of the road may be observed two very fine silver firs, remarkable, not only for their size, but for their large, peculiarly formed and crooked branches. One of them is known as the "marriage tree" from the circumstance of two of the branches, originally separate, having become united into one. Just at this point, 8 miles from Tarbert, the road turns away from the loch, and cutting across the promontory of Ardpatrick (where tradition asserts St. Patrick landed on certain of his journeyings between Scotland and Ireland), approaches the sea again at the head of Loch Stornoway. As we pass along towards this latter point, we may note that at a distance of half-an-hour's walk from Carse stables, through the rough moorland, a loch, known as Loch-a-Bhaillidh is reached, which is of interest as containing one of those crannogs or lake-dwellings formerly referred to. The loch is lonely and secluded, and it is situated 326 feet above sea-level. The estate of Carse is owned by John Birkmyre, Junr., Esq.

THE OLD SCHOOL-HOUSE, LOCHEND.

The Hill of the Black Hound.

Between Dunmore and Loch-a-Bhaillidh there is a pyramidal hill which bears the name of Dun-na-choindhuibh (the Hill of the Black Hound). This hill is crowned by the remains of an old fort, which was at one time the residence of a famous hunter and cateran named Torquil Mor, who was the possessor of a great boar-hound, named *Luath*, or the swift one.

From this boar-hound the bill received its name. Torquil was the Rob Roy of Knapdale, and with his hand of broken men, desperate fellows whom he had often to admonish with a stroke of his sword, he drove many a creach from far afield to the dreary solitudes around Loch-a-Bhaillidh.

Reckless though he was, and implacable to his foes, Torquil could, when called upon by the needy, act the part of a generous friend. On one occasion he was appealed to by a poor widow whose husband had been slain by a band of caterans, and her cattle swept away from field and hillside. Within a week, Torquil brought to the poor woman two cows for every one she had lost, and, in addition, the head of the man who had slain her husband.

But though Torquil was brave and, on occasion, generous, he was also very superstitious, and had a great regard for a celebrated witch known as *Cailleach Mhor na Craig*, the big woman of Craig. With her he was often in consultation, and to her machinations he attributed much of his success. Anxious to know his ultimate fate, he again and again importuned her to reveal it to him. After long resistance she yielded, telling him that he would be killed in battle, "but not the battle of men." "Look with me beyond the veil. I see you; but, alas! how changed! . . . Your spear lies broken by your side, where also lies your enemy."

According to tradition, Torquil met his death in the hunting of a monster boar, which lesser men than the mighty hunter had failed to dislodge from the fastnesses of Torr-an-Tuirc. From morn till eve, Torquil, accompanied by his trusty hound, followed the arduous chase, driving the great beast along the hillside and through the dense wood of Craig, till, as night drew on, it sought refuge in the ruinous fort of Dunmore. Arrived on the scene, Torquil found his faithful hound in its death agony, mangled and torn. In an instant, the spear of the hunter was driven deep into the flank of the boar. Rushing madly through a gap in the wall (Torquil still holding to the spear) the infuriated beast, unable to stay its wild career, dashed over the precipitous rock on which the fort stood, dragging Torquil with him. And thus died the great boar, and with it, Torquil Mor, the last tenant of Dun-na-choin-dhuibh.

Slaughter of the Clan Iver

The mansion-house of Ardpatrick, the residence of Captain J. C. Campbell, R.N., is situated well out on the promontory which gives its name to the estate. This headland, which rises to a height of 265 feet, stands guard to the loch on the Kilberry side as Dunskeig does on the Kintyre shore. The estate is beautifully wooded, the trees flourishing with great luxuriance.

Close by the head of Loch Stornoway, and on a flat delta formed by a stream which falls into the bay, may be seen three standing stones, the largest of which reaches to a height of 10 feet. Close by are the Parish Church of Kilberry, built in 1821, and the "Churchyard of the McIvers." The following tradition is associated with the churchyard:—

Once upon a time the Clan Iver, bent on "lifting" the cattle of the Campbells who resided in this neighbourhood, encamped for the night where the great stones stand. Learning their purpose, the Campbells ambushed themselves behind a small hill known by the appropriate name of Sròn á Mhionnan (the knoll of the curse or

IN ARHAINN-NAN-GILLEAN GLEN.

imprecation). In the dress of a mendicant minstrel, the leader of the Campbells entered the camp of the McIvers singing songs and reciting ballads. None knew him for what he was, and when he had learned all he desired to know he took his departure. In the middle of the night, when the McIvers were fast asleep, the Campbells issued from their hiding place, and fell upon the slumberers, all of whom were killed except two. These fled for their lives, but one was overtaken and slain about three miles from Carse, and the other fell into the stream when crossing Abhainn-nan-Gillean, and there he was killed. Most of the bodies were buried within the graveyard, and so it got its name "Earrann Chlann Imheir," the portion of the Clan Iver.

Kilberry estate, which derives its name from the old church or cell, which was dedicated to St. Berach, is the property of John Campbell, Esq., Convener of the County, who resides in Kilberry Castle. The old castle, founded as far back as 1497, was burned in 1778 by Paul Jones, the pirate. The baptismal name of this noted sea rover was John Paul. He was the son of a gardener of the same name, and was born at Kirkbean about the year 1747. Kilberry Castle was entirely rebuilt in 1844, and was enlarged in 1871.

We have now reached the end of our journey (14 miles), but it should be noted that by prolonging our tour in the direction we have been travelling, Tarbert may be reached again without retracing our steps. This circular trip, which is known as the drive round Ormsary, brings us to the village by the Ardrishaig road. It extends to 40 miles, and as it passes by the sides of West Loch Tarbert, Loch Caolisport, and Loch Fyne, it constitutes a delightful excursion. Inns will be found at Lairgnahunsion (11 miles), and Achahoish (20 miles), and postal and telegraph offices at the latter hamlet, and at Kilberry. Achahoish Inn is situated at the head of Loch Caolisport. In this neighbourhood, King Connal, one of the earliest of the Dalriadic kings, and a friend of St. Columba, had, for a time, his residence. There he is said to have been visited by the Saint on the occasion when he conferred upon Columba the gift of Iona. A curious cave chapel at Cove, on the shore of the loch, is traditionally said to have been Columba's first church in Scotland. In the cave is a rock altar, and a cross is carved on the wall beyond. On the upper surface of the altar a circular font has been hewn out of the rock, and a drip from the roof of the cave serves to keep the font constantly supplied with fresh water.

The door of memory opens wide as we tread these

loch-indented shores, so fair, so grandly picturesque, so historically interesting, and yet so unknown to the tourist race. The day is surely not far distant when this romantically beautiful portion of the seaboard of Argyll, at present so isolated and removed from the beaten track, will be brought into more intimate relationship with the great centres of population. This, it is probable, will be best effected by placing a steamer on these western seas which will traverse Loch Caolisport and Loch Sween, and connect with the Royal Route at West Tarbert and Crinan. When this alluring vision becomes indeed a reality, few trips over Scottish waters will compare in grandeur and sublimity with the sail on these four fair lochs—West Loch Tarbert, Loch Caolisport, Loch Sween, and Loch Crinan—and over the island-strewed seas of this region of the west.

> Westward away! westward away!
> When summer is calling on moorland and brae;
> When the wind blows soft o'er the Hebrid Isles,
> And the old sea is wreathed in rippling smiles,
> And the mountain lone and the bracken-glen
> Whisper of rest for weary men:
>   Westward away! away!
>
> Westward away! westward away!
> To the dear old home by the rock-girt bay;
> Where white wings flit o'er the foam-tipped tide,
> And the proud skiff foots it with jaunty stride;
> Where comrades are hearty and leal and true,
> And a welcome is waiting for me and for you:
>   Westward away! away!

TARBERT — LOCH FYNE.

THE COLUMBA HOTEL.

THE PRINCIPAL HOTEL FOR TOURISTS

DELIGHTFULLY situated at Pier and adjacent to Golf Course. Fishing good. The accommodation and cuisine equal the best to be found.

BILLIARDS.

D. SUTHERLAND,
PROPRIETOR.

WILLIAM M'MILLAN,

Motor Launch Builder,

TARBERT.

New and Second-Hand	REPAIRS OF EVERY DESCRIPTION PROMPTLY DONE.
Motor Launches	
For Sale or Hire.	MOTOR CAR ACCUMULATORS CHARGED At Moderate Prices.

List of Houses at the New Golf Course to Let for Season sent on application.

126

PETER McPHERSON

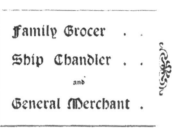

Family Grocer . .

Ship Chandler . .

and

General Merchant .

HARBOUR STREET,

TARBERT.

Fishing Gear, Nets, Ropes, Fishermen's Clothing, etc., etc.

FAMILIES AND YACHTS SUPPLIED AT LOWEST CUT PRICES.

Orders Called for and Delivered Daily.

"Highland Spring"

BOTTLED

AND

SOLD

AT

TARBERT, LOCH FYNE.

Incomparably superior to the ordinary run of Table Waters
on account of Excellent Spring Water and Pure
Materials used in Manufacture.

130

Alexander Mitchell,

FAMILY GROCER,

DRAPER, IRONMONGER, AND GENERAL HOUSE FURNISHER,

HARBOUR STREET. TARBERT.

High-Class Family Groceries and Provisions.	LARGE SELECTION OF FANCY GOODS COMPRISING Souvenirs, Crested China, Stationery, Purses, Photo Frames, Glass and China Ornaments, Toys, &c.	House Coals delivered in Quantity or in Bags.

Fishing Rods and Tackle.   Table Cutlery.
Catering for Shooting Lodges and Yachts a Speciality
All kinds of Spratt's Game Meal and Dog
Feeding supplied.

THE EMPORIUM, ...

 TARBERT, Loch Fyne.

.. FOR ..

MILLINERY, GENERAL DRAPERY,

FANCY GOODS, WOOLS, NEEDLEWORK

LADIES' AND CHILDREN'S

BOOTS, SHOES, and SLIPPERS.

M. & C. LAMONT.

THOMSON'S

TEMPERANCE HOTEL,

TARBERT.

Comfortable Accommodation ...

... at Moderate Rates.

DINNERS.   ·.·   TEAS, &c.

134

A. M. DICKIE, 🥢

Yacht, Motor Launch,
AND
General Boat Builder,

TARBERT.

YACHT SLIP.　∴　YACHTS WINTERED.
GOOD DRY STORE.

. . REPAIRS . .
OI EVERY DESCRIPTION at MODERATE TERMS.

MOTOR LAUNCHES FOR SALE OR HIRE.

MACLEOD'S CARTRIDGES

FOR THE SHOOTING SEASON.

Loaded with E.C., Schultze, Kynoch, Amberite, Ballastite, Empire, or other Nito Powders, and with Chilled Shot any size from No. 12 to Swan Shot.

Cases of the undernoted guage always in stock—12, 14, 16, 20, 28, 410.

Prices as under, usual charge (42 grains and 1 or 1¼ oz. shot—

Grouse Cases, loaded		...	**11/6 per 100**	
Waterproof ,,	,,		**10/6**	,,
Best Paper, ,,	,,		**10/**	,,
Club	,,	,,	**8/6**	,,

A Special Offer to Gamekeepers and Farmers

A Reliable Smokeless Cartridge ; Specially Loaded by MACLEOD at Tarbert, and suitable for Shooting on Sea or Land. Usual Loading. Any number of Shot.

AT 6/6 PER 100. CASH WITH ORDER.
Booking Extra. Freight Paid on 500. TRY THEM.

Factory Loaded Cartridges in Stock at Makers' Advertised Prices.

Rifle Cartridges of all bore, loaded with Black or Smokeless Powder, always in Stock.

Collapsible and Rigid Game Boxes for 1, 2, and 3 brace.

Game and Cartridge Bags, Dog Collars, Leads, Muzzles, Whips, Calls, &c. A large and select stock of Fishing Tackle for Loch and Burn Fishing in Flies, Casts, Hooks, Rods, &c.

Selections sent on application to choose from.

All Orders sent on receipt of Letter or Wire.

Sportsmen should call and see our large and varied Stock of all ☞ SPORTING REQUISITES. ☜

PRATT'S SHELL MOTOR SPIRIT KEPT IN STOCK.

ADDRESS—MACLEOD. GUNSMITH. TARBERT.